For Chuck

THE IDEA OF
A MENTAL ILLNESS

by Marshall Edelson, M.D., Ph.D.

SOCIAL STUDIES LIBRARY,
SOCIAL STUDIES CENTRE, GEORGE ST
OXFORD. OX1 2RL

WITHDRAWN

38525

SOCIAL STUDIES
LIBRARY.
45. WELLINGTON SQUARE,
OXFORD

WITHDRAWN

New Haven and London, Yale University Press, 1971

Copyright © 1971 by Yale University.
All rights reserved. This book may not be
reproduced, in whole or in part, in any form
(except by reviewers for the public press),
without written permission from the publishers.
Library of Congress catalog card number: 71-140527.
International standard book number: 0-300-01430-9.

Designed by Sally Sullivan
and set in IBM Selectric Press Roman type.
Printed in the United States of America by
The Carl Purington Rollins Printing-Office
of the Yale University Press.

Distributed in Great Britain, Europe, and Africa by
Yale University Press, Ltd., London; in Canada by
McGill-Queen's University Press, Montreal; in Mexico
by Centro Interamericano de Libros Académicos,
Mexico City; in Central and South America by Kaiman
& Polon, Inc., New York City; in Australasia by
Australia and New Zealand Book Co., Pty., Ltd.,
Artarmon, New South Wales; in India by UBS Publishers'
Distributors Pvt., Ltd., Delhi; in Japan by John
Weatherhill, Inc., Tokyo.

Contents

Introduction   1

1. What Is Man?   7

2. The Idea of a Mental Illness   38

3. Symbolic Process and Consciousness   73

4. The Treatment of a Mental Illness   105

References   137

Introduction

The following pages represent the acts of my own mind as I try to make sense of the psychiatric enterprise. They involve first of all a dialogue, at some points an argument, with myself. They are also addressed to any reader—physician, psychiatrist, psychoanalyst, psychologist, psychotherapist, student—who cares to listen in, or join me in my quest and questioning. Since the thoughts expressed and recorded here belong to this moment in time, to a stage in my own problem-solving, I do not accept any responsibility for defending them as either systematic or complete. I make no pretense at an orderly, direct, concise presentation, because such a presentation would be in fact a false representation. Expect, then, obscure statements, awkward statements, and obvious statements; trite passages and thick passages; colloquialisms and technical language. Expect meandering from the point, digressions, asides, lines of thought picked up, dropped, and left—not to be picked up again in these pages, perhaps not again for months or years, if ever. It cannot be otherwise, if I am to let you know how I muddle along in approaching problems in my own field at a time that is, hopefully, nearer the beginning of my work than its end. If you do not like to wander, wondering, trying to work things out, put this book down now.

I should say here also that, although I make much reference to schizophrenia, this book is not about schizophrenia. It is about ways of thinking, illustrated here in a presentation of ways of thinking about schizophrenia. I do not believe that there is much to learn about schizophrenia from these pages, but it is my hope that there is something to be learned about how a psychiatrist thinks about man, about the nature of mental illness, and about the treatment of mental illness. If I compare, for example, the views on schizophrenia of Freud with those of Federn and Pious, it is not primarily out of regard to the final merits of these points of view either in relation to each other or in relation to other points of view not even described, but because these views to some extent may stand for ways of approaching one problem in psychiatry and, therefore, other problems as well.

I imagine some readers will be offended by the casual way in which I wonder, as I examine Freud's model of mental illness, what this or that concept of his might be like formulated from a perspective other than the positivism that gave the concept its form in his theory-building. I do not intend here any careful, thorough, scholarly reexamination of psychoanalytic theory. Nor do I intend simplistically to rip Freud's ideas from the context his entire theoretical work gives to them, nor to add confusion to this field by holding on to his words while redefining them to suit my own theoretical and rhetorical purposes. However, I have sensed that Freud's effort to make the study of psychological phenomena respectable to the science of his time may have led him to some physicalistic formulations that appear now as almost incongruous impositions upon his great empirical discoveries, which are essentially one discovery, the discovery of psychic reality. How would Freud have formulated his explanations of psychological phenomena in a time such as ours, when the recognition of man as a symbolizing animal—the acknowledgment of the significance of symbolic process, perhaps especially of language, of the world of value as well as the world of fact, and of the problem of meaning for understanding man's actions, social life, and the nature of his mind—has become almost a commonplace, and the influence of the canons and dicta of positivism upon science wanes? This book is a small part of a larger inquiry that seeks the conceptual means to bridge the gap between Freud's scientific Zeitgeist and that of our own (in fact, he is one of the important shapers of our own Zeitgeist), without sacrifice or erosion of his major achievements.

I am involved here not with questions of "true" or "false," but with shifts from one frame of reference or perspective to another. The implications of the terms of a theory are often revealed by viewing the theory from a ground at least in part outside it, by wrenching its terms from their usual setting and placing them with resulting incongruity in a new one. Since ideas are free inventions, I am not reluctant to play with them, combining perspectives violently and discovering faults that form along the lines where points of view diverge and converge.

I have used the lecture form, partly because it seemed to me well suited to the purpose of thinking aloud, and partly in obvious, though of course imperfect, emulation of the style of Freud's *Introductory Lectures.* I make this confession in acknowledgment of my admiration, even though I realize that such a confession burdens this small work with a comparison to the work of a master rhetorician from which it must certainly suffer.

The title is a paraphrase of the title of Peter Winch's book *The Idea of a Social Science* (London: Routledge and Kegan Paul; New York: Humanities Press, 1958). This book was brought to my attention by my excellent and most helpful editor, Jane Isay, after she read these pages; she is correct, I think, in feeling some kinship of interest and idea between the two books.

I am grateful to Dr. Hans Loewald for his interest in my ideas and his thoughtful discussions of them; he encouraged me to write these lectures in a time and place somewhat inhospitable to the formal lecture and he also suggested they be published. Although hesitant because of their "work in progress" quality, I welcome their publication partly for the opportunity afforded to call attention to the influence of Dr. William Pious, whose teaching at the Western New England Institute for Psychoanalysis has been a source of inspiration for my thinking about some of the problems discussed here. The relation between Wallace Stevens' views about reality and imagination and those of Freud about rationality and psychic reality, mentioned in the first lecture, was first discussed with Dr. Henry Wexler. There are reminiscences in the second lecture of discussions with Dr. Albert Solnit and Dr. Samuel Ritvo about the transference neurosis and the importance of a focus upon psychic reality in psychoanalytic work, and with Dr. Seymour Lustman about research in psychoanalysis. I am indebted to Dr. Theodore Lidz for many benefactions, including his close, patient reading of an earlier version of this work in manuscript and his comments which helped me to see more clearly what I was up to in writing it.

The reader who is familiar with my previous work will recognize that I continue in these lectures lines of thought begun, from one starting point, in *The Termination of Intensive Psychotherapy* (Springfield, Ill.: Charles C. Thomas, 1963), and, from another, in the section "A Prologue to Curriculum: Symbolism and System," of Chapter 2, "The Integration of the Behavioral

Sciences and Clinical Experience in Teaching Medical Students," in *Training Tomorrow's Psychiatrist,* edited by Theodore Lidz and Marshall Edelson (New Haven: Yale University Press, 1970). Some paragraphs from that section, in somewhat different form, are woven into the first of these lectures. The same reader may wonder that I did not include lectures on sociotherapy as well as psychotherapy in considering the treatment of schizophrenia. Such lectures would of necessity have consisted largely of excerpts from recent work—namely, *Sociotherapy and Psychotherapy* (Chicago: University of Chicago, 1970) and *The Practice of Sociotherapy: A Case Study* (New Haven: Yale University Press, 1970) —and are therefore not included here.

1: What Is Man?

Ladies and gentlemen:

What is man? A more modest inquiry: what answer does a physician, more specifically a psychiatrist, give to the question what is man?

Some of you, perhaps unwittingly, are inclined to answer: man is a thing. Like all other things, he can be explained ultimately by the categories and methods of physical science. For you, consideration of the subjective experience of man is vaguely disreputable, or, more sternly, contrary to the canons of empirical science. What shall a physician, a scientist, have to do with subjective experience, which, after all, is a mere epiphenomenon of such objective observable matters as heredity and environment?

You might add to your definition of man: man is reactive. He reacts to heredity and environment. His behavior is caused by, is a reaction to, hereditary endowment, environmental stimuli, or a combination of these.

Another part of your answer is likely to be: man is rational. That is, if you admit subjective elements for consideration at all, and then only most unwillingly, you will admit such elements in the form of reason. You will imagine that man's behavior is determined by valid empirical knowledge. If behavior fails to be rational, it is because man is in error (his knowledge is mistaken) or because man is ignorant (he does not yet possess the knowledge he needs to behave rationally).

You are certainly safe in introducing this subjective element. Why is man ignorant or in error? It all goes back to limitations imposed by his heredity or distortions imposed by his environment. These are part of the objective realm of things and can be safely studied. On the other hand, if man behaves rationally, his behavior is a perfect match of, an adaptation to, his objective situation—the body he is born with or the environment in which he lives. Of course, as you have realized already, that heredity and that environment can be studied without recourse to any subjective frame of reference.

This man you have described, what makes him go? It is convenient to assume that he is motivated by a chaos of unrelated wants, preferably consequences of the workings of the machinery of his body, which push him to behavior that satisfies. Such behavior is governed, if by anything subjective, by considerations of rational self-interest. In this connection, you would refuse to allow us to become interested in ends or goals of behavior as inhabiting or making up the mind of man, lest we find ourselves succumbing to entelechial or vitalistic mythologies or even beginning to discourse about the soul. For how can a scientific man take such a notion as mind seriously? So, let us assume that the ends or goals of behavior are random, without significant relation to each other; therefore it is not necessary to consider them in themselves. Ends or goals are chosen because of—but you cannot use a word such as chosen, which is, in the framework of your answer, a meaningless word—rather, ends or goals are *determined by* empirical knowledge of the past and present, of the objective situation. Therefore, such ends or goals may be essentially reduced to the characteristics of that objective situation, a situation made up of things that may be investigated objectively. Again, we are saved from any need to become involved in a subjective frame of reference.

Naturally, such a view of man is, in a sense, optimistic, as well as deterministic. Man's future is foretold. He may be judged according to his position on a fixed ladder of progress. His history consists of evolutionary progress in a linear process toward a foreseeable culmination. For, if man is rational—if his behavior is determined by a rational understanding of his objective situation—then, since ignorance and error are progressively eliminated by the accumulation of scientific knowledge and techniques, evolution must be linear and progressive.

However, you will surely try to persuade me that we might just as well forget about rationality along with other objectionable subjective factors. For, after all, since hereditary variations are automatically selected in terms of adaptation to environmental conditions, and since there is automatic environmental conditioning of events according to what is rewarded, then adaptation must improve; that is to say, evolution must be linear and progressive.

There is another answer to the question, what is man? We might say there is an anti-answer, as though the two answers exist primarily to oppose each other, one depending on the existence of the other for its meaning. These two answers are not only answers to the question, what is man? They are answers to each other. Some of you will recognize the idealistic conception of man, which argues with the more respectable, scientifically speaking, positivistic conception of man we have just put forth.

This answer begins, awkwardly enough, with the statement: man is lived by the idea. His actions are emanations, embodiments, or expressions of ideas, values, or ideals. Nonsubjective elements, the objective conditions of behavior such as heredity or environment, are irrelevant. Rationality is irrelevant. Behavior expresses meaning or is a manifestation of timeless ideas. Man is, in this view, irreducibly qualitatively individual. Since every man, and indeed every group and every society, is a unique manifestation and historical phenomenon, the behavior of any such entity cannot become the basis for analysis, generalization, and prediction. Its meaning can only be grasped intuitively and as a whole. Of course, then, man's history is a succession of unrelated, unique events—manifestations or objectifications (in different places, at different times) of different ideas or ideals. The concept of progress is inapplicable.

This conception of man claims our attention because it is an inseparable shadow or obverse side of the positivistic conception. However, those of us who are interested in the practice of scientific medicine and in scientific investigation—that is, in classification, hypotheses, generalization, and empirical verification—have difficulty with this conception, feeling, on the one hand, uneasily that it is attractively allied to a concern with the individual as a unique phenomenon and not just an illustration of the general case, and, on the other, that such a view, if seriously adopted, might throw us out of business as physicians and scientists.

Some of you are no doubt already ahead of me. Certainly, if we have an answer and an anti-answer to the question, what is man? then we may expect a third possible answer that, in some sense, grows out of and yet transcends the opposition of the first two.

This answer begins, in the words of Ernst Cassirer, with the proposition: man is the *animal symbolicum.* Again, in the words of Kenneth Burke, man is "the animal that makes, uses and misuses symbols." The symbolization function is man's unique characteristic, emerging at his level of biological organization.

Symbol is a central term for this view of man. Yet I am not at all sure how to define symbol. For present purposes, tentatively, shall we consider an entity to be a symbol to the extent that it is formulative, abstractive, and suasive?

An entity is formulative if it gives distinctive form to experience. A symbol does not simply arise out of experience, as an extract or summary of it. A symbol is rather an invention that is imposed upon, or composes, experience. It is a conception of reality, not a sign of it. A symbol is a way of experiencing, a selection from among alternative ways of experiencing or alternative orientations to experience, each with distinctive characteristics, aims, or consequences. Symbolization, the generation of symbols, is essential to human experience; it is the process by which knowledge of reality is mediated at the human level of biological organization.

An entity is abstractive if its meaning is not exhausted by reference to the immediate presence of a concrete reality, specific object, or actual instance; if it expresses qualities or characteristics apart from their embodiment in any specific object or actual instance; or if it represents an essence, a concentration of what is essential of something more general or complex, or a concentration of what is shared by more than one object or instance. A crucial characteristic of a symbol is that it always implies something beyond, and is in this sense independent of, any immediate experience. A symbol refers to the imagined, to the invisible, to the negative. A symbol is a recreation of the past or a procreation of the future. A symbol reminds, anticipates, or implies, rather than indicates, signals, or announces. A symbol may stand for, represent, evoke, or imply some other entity by virtue of a property, quality, characteristic, or participation in some event it shares with that otherwise different entity; or it may symbolize another entity by virtue of an arbitrary, conventional link to it, that is, by agreement.

An entity is suasive when, as a component of personality or social systems, it exerts effects independent of any capacities for physical force it possesses.

An entity that conveys symbolic meaning has symbolic and nonsymbolic aspects. In its nonsymbolic aspects, it is the vehicle or medium through which the symbolic meaning is objectified or achieves concrete form. A symbolic form is an organization of such entities, embodying a particular orientation, or giving a particular distinctive form, to experience. Language, myth, religion, law, art, and science are examples of symbolic forms.

Symbolic process may refer either to the generation of symbolic forms or to the vicissitudes or effects of such symbolic forms, in a personality system or—when these forms are shared by interacting persons—in a social system.

Cassirer tends to view the primary function of the symbol as formulative. It is a creation, a conception of reality, which composes experience. The symbol makes it possible to hold on to, to imagine, and to think about aspects of reality in their absence.

Burke tends to view the primary function of the symbol as suasive—communicative and instrumental. It is used in discourse to transmit and exchange ideas, to explain, persuade, arouse, sanction. Ultimately, it is an instrument for the satisfaction of wants and the control of resources (especially the cooperation of other humans) required for such satisfaction.

The symbol may be held, in the first view, to impose upon reality a conception of it; the symbol "presents" that conception in some form. Freud's emphasis upon the determinative role of psychic reality is an example. If the second view is coupled with a naive realism— which, to add to our difficulty, it appears to be elsewhere in Freud's writing—then the symbol may be held to represent an actual aspect of reality out there, an object or relation between objects to which the symbol may be linked by convention, but which is considered to have some true existence apart from any symbolization of it.

According to Cassirer, the methods of introspection and observation of behavior are inadequate for the understanding of man as a symbolizing animal. One must also consider the works of man, his culture, which constitute the symbolic world of his own making, and reveal by inference the nature of their maker.

In studying the works of man, Cassirer makes a clear distinction between a concern with the genesis of a symbolic form (how did it arise in the course of time? from what precursors?) and the systematic, structural-functional analysis of the symbolic form, which establishes what is logically though not necessarily prior. The functions of a symbolic form, the aims it realizes, may be reconstructed from an analysis of its structure, as one might seek to reconstruct the special modes of experience of each kind of organism from its anatomical structure.

Cassirer's differentiation of two types of thinking, the mythic and the rational-discursive, bears an obvious relationship (which has been pointed out, for example, by Langer) to Freud's great discovery of primary and secondary process, achieved by different methods and in a different empirical realm. Language has close links in its origins to mythic thinking; it develops into a form that is also capable of employment in rational-discursive thinking.

(I wonder why Cassirer ignored to such an extent the work of Freud? A number of reasons are suggested by passing comments in his work. He distrusted the method of introspection and the focus upon a single individual as a way of answering questions about the nature of man as a symbolizing animal. He apparently had misread Freud or was not familiar with much of his writing—either possibility surprising in a scholar of such erudition—and believed that Freud explained everything by a single factor: sex. He was critical of the concept "instinct," particularly pretensions to explanation by use of such a concept, and apparently did not understand that Freud had something psychical in mind in using such a concept. Finally, perhaps most important, Cassirer emphasized the sacred rather than pleasure as essential in mythic thinking. It is certainly in his emphasis on the reflex reduction of tension and pleasure that Freud betrays his ties to a utilitarian positivism. For Cassirer, the quality of sacredness arises out of man's fear of death; it is an assertion of immortality, continuity, and the solidarity of the universe; it functions to arouse man to search, to strive, and to realize possibility.)

In addition to the protosymbolic forms of myth and language, Cassirer discusses four works of man—religion, art, history, and science. These, he believes, have a unity as symbolic forms, but differences in structure and function. For Cassirer, art is a prototype of the symbolic world of sensuous forms, creating order in apprehension; science is a prototype of the symbolic world of cognitive forms, the world of space, time, and causality, creating order in comprehension; history is a prototype of the symbolic world of moral judgment, the world in which man seeks to understand himself and the consequences of his social actions, creating order in social relations; and religion is the prototype of the symbolic world of sacred conceptions or ideals, creating order in man's orientations to the future and his strivings to realize the possibilities he conceives.

You may be as interested as I am to notice that there are parallels in this formulation with Talcott Parsons' differentiation of four subsystems—goal-attainment, adaptation, integration, and pattern-maintenance—of any system of action, and Freud's differentiation of four subsystems of personalities (I say four, because of my preference for distinguishing between superego and ego-ideal as functional subsystems)—id, ego, superego, and ego-ideal. The parallel may be more than a coincidence. Do you think it may arise from the involvement of each of these thinkers in a consideration of symbolic processes?

Although Cassirer clearly means that different symbolic forms are not comparable (i.e., subject to the same standards), entering as they do into the creation of distinct symbolic worlds with different structures and functions, he nevertheless on occasion describes myth and magic as false and erroneous forms of symbolic thought, which pave the way to the true symbolism of modern science. This is similar to the rationalistic bias of Freud, which occasionally leads him into an equation of ego with health and "true" reality. As a scientist rooted in positivistic tradition, Freud tended to take "reality" for granted as a concept, in the same way that as a Victorian he took "values" for granted and, focusing on moral values, was not moved to distinguish between kinds of values or to realize that his own passion for truth was itself commitment to a value standard competing with other value standards. Freud did not bother to see or make explicit that the objective reality of the rational ego—created according to the reality principle—is as much a result of an act of the mind as the inner world of psychic reality he so brilliantly revealed, its phantasmagoria created according to the pleasure principle. He eschewed philosophical questions when these touched on the conceptual equipment he accepted as given. So, Wallace Stevens, in defense of imagination as a necessary agent—in interaction with the brute, bare, essentially unknowable rock of reality—for the creation of any reality apprehendable and comprehendable by man, is able to make the following bitter comments, paradoxically enough, about Freud, the discoverer of psychic reality, the archeologist of the imagination at work in the creation of reality:

Boileau's remark that Descartes had cut poetry's throat is a remark that could have been made respecting a great many people during the last hundred years, and of no one more aptly than of Freud, who, as it happens, was familiar with it and repeats it in his *Future of an Illusion.* [I could not discover such a reference in that essay.] The object of that essay was to suggest a surrender to reality. His premise was that it is the unmistakable character of the present situation not that the promises of religion have become smaller but that they appear less credible to people.

He notes the decline of religious belief and disagrees with the argument that man cannot in general do without the consolation of what he calls the religious illusion and that without it he would not endure the cruelty of reality. His conclusion is that man must venture at last into the hostile world and that this may be called education to reality. There is much more in that essay inimical to poetry and not least the observation in one of the final pages that "The voice of the intellect is a soft one, but it does not rest until it has gained a hearing." This, I fear, is intended to be the voice of the realist.

Kenneth Burke has emphasized rather than the formulative the communicative function of the symbol. He has distinguished between a scientistic or epistemological view of symbol as a form of knowledge and a dramatistic view of symbol as a form of action. The development of symbolization, if not its origin, is shaped by communicative necessities. However, a symbol is not merely a purveyor of information, of definition and description, but is rather intrinsically hortatory, symbolic action; even the names of things are programs suggesting attitudes and acts. Language is a mode of persuasion, a means by which men obtain cooperation of one another. Mind is largely a linguistic product, constructed of social realities—patterns of cooperation—and the communicative materials creating and maintaining such patterns.

Motives, according to Burke, are intrinsic to language and essentially another name for it. (Just as Burke in our day is able to write that motives and language are one, so Lévi-Strauss in another realm, emphasizing, however, the formulative function of symbolization, writes essentially that society—and its institutions—and language are one: both are manifestations of ways of ordering and classifying experience; both are forms or objectifications of thought.)

Communication between parts of a system arises because, although such parts must function together (that is, cooperate) as members of the same system, they are yet—as individuated, differentiated parts—divided. This combination of division and consubstantiality is the necessary condition of communication. Symbols are one means of communication. A symbol as suasive entity is intrinsically concerned with, intrinsically a mode of response to, division. The relation of a symbol to other symbols defines a particular strategy for mitigating or operating upon division.

Communication, when it involves the suasive effects of symbols participating in a personality or social system, is that change (in response to division or partition in the system) wrought in the system (for example, in the relation between two parts or in the state of one part that is in relation to another) by a symbol (that is, by the generation and presentation of a conception) in so far as such a symbol reminds, anticipates, implies, evokes, or appeals to certain grounds for such change; the implicit or explicit relation of such a symbol to other symbols defines a strategy—intrinsic to symbolicity—for operating upon division. A symbol is suasive in so far as it motivates action by reminding, anticipating, implying, evoking, adducing, locating, or appealing to certain grounds (reasons or motives) for such action, and in so far as it participates in relation to other symbols in a particular strategy for mitigating or operating upon division.

What are the grounds for action to which a symbol

appeals, which it implies, which it locates? Burke's primary method is the study of literary forms; using a dramatistic terminology, he refers to five loci of motives: scene, agent, agency, purpose, act.

No matter which of these elements is explicitly named, the others are also implied. The implications of a symbol as a suasive entity or symbolic act are analogous to those an axiom or set of axioms, all contained within it that may be deduced or made explicit from it. For example, Burke suggests that use of such a term or concept as "repression" (*act*) implies or inevitably leads to such terms or concepts as: 1) a repressing *agent;* 2) that which is repressed or to be repressed with a degree of failure or success to which is associated pain or pleasure (*purpose*); 3) the pressure or energy used to carry out the act of repression (*agency*); 4) an unconscious—the location of the repressed (*scene*). Any one of these terms leads to all the others. A symbol as a suasive entity or symbolic act is, then, a tautology, a structure of elements or terms in which each part is implicit in all parts.

Motive is an abbreviated title for "conception of a complex action." If one knows a man's conception, one knows how he will act or why he acts as he does. The conception is the motive for action. A symbol may locate a motive for action in the characteristics of a *scene* in which action occurs; or in the characteristics of an *agent* of action. A symbol may locate a motive for action in its beginnings, in an *agency*—a resource or potentiality for action; or a symbol may locate a motive for action in its culmination, in the fulfillment or use of potentialities in consummation or realization of *purpose.*

There are also motives or grounds for action located in

man's devotion to the symbol systems he uses. Such devotion to the symbol enhances the symbol's intrinsic capacity to mitigate or operate upon division. A symbol has implications. Every language implies possible developments. For a symbolizing animal, following out such implications, carrying out these terministic possibilities in action becomes an end in itself, irrespective of other consequences such action may have. Such action may appear peremptory or compelled, since all things implied have to be developed; all the implications of a terminology have to be tracked down with a kind of formal thoroughness; all the implications of a key term have to be exhausted. Once man is committed to a conception, to a language, to a symbol or symbol system, he acts to bring his life into conformity with it; he models his life after it; he governs his life by the pursuit and realization of its implications. He persuades others to act in such a way that he may make himself and his world over in the image of his language. Therefore, Burke states, paradoxically, that things are the signs of words, not words the signs of things. "The spirit of words is infused into or symbolized by nonverbal things," rather than "a word is learned as the sign of a thing." (Wallace Stevens writes: "Life is the reflection of literature.")

I remind you that motive and action as used in the preceding paragraphs should be distinguished from the motion or reaction resulting from the "physicality" of man and the effect of physical forces upon him (as in "falling down a hill") as well as from the behavior or reactions resulting from the "animality" of man (that are solely effects of physiological processes unmediated by symbolic process). It is a fallacy to attribute consequences of symbolicity to physicality or animality.

Man's devotion to his symbols and symbol systems is a manifestation of his "rage for order." ("Man," says Burke, "is moved by a sense of order.") Disorder is represented by division without consubstantiality. Then communication is impossible. Division is mitigated by preserving and organizing it, or by transcending it, through resources intrinsic to symbolicity. Symbols and symbol systems are intrinsically resources for the creation of order. Order is born out of the implications of symbols, their relations to each other, and is a consequence of any use of symbols.

Symbols have entelechial implications, because symbols, which are generated by abstraction, have a tendency to suggest or anticipate ideals—perfect, more abstract forms. Such ideals transcend divisions or differences through movement to higher or prior, more inclusive or more essential, conceptions. The entelechial implications of a symbol create through such transcendence a particular kind of order. Development is temporal or hierarchic (in time or in essence) progressive or regressive succession. An essence is carried up or down, forward or backward, to an apotheosis of excess. Continuity, composition, and the fulfillment or reinforcement of a given pattern, are emphasized. Such a principle of order serves as grounds for action: in preoccupations in terms of which everything—no matter how seemingly disparate—is interpreted; in the continual search for materials that, no matter how incongruous, are fused and made to link with or belong to such a preoccupation (what Burke, following Dewey, calls, for example, an "occupational psychosis"); in the purposive shaping of later experience in terms of some early, primal experience; and in the sacrifices made on the altar of "a way." ("Man," says Burke, "is goaded by the

spirit of hierarchy, and rotten with perfection." The
hierarchic incentive is not just a function of social institutions, but is "embedded in the very nature of language.")

Symbols have admonitory implications, because symbols, which are conceptions of the imagined, the invisible, the negative, manifest the ability of the symbolizing animal to say "no" in the presence of "yes."
("Man," says Burke, "is the inventor of the negative, is
moralized by the negative.") Admonitory implications
are illustrated by the tendency of a certain kind of symbol to imply its antithesis, to require its antithesis for
adequate definition of itself. The admonitory implications of a symbol create through such antitheses,
through dissociations, discontinuities, and differentia-
tions, a particular kind of order. Development is dia-
lectical. Division is preserved and organized: opposites
check, caution, and correct each other; harmony is in
the balance of opposites, in the arrangement of differences, in the tension of conflict. Such a principle of
order serves as grounds for action in choice, selection
between alternatives, efforts at integration or adaptation. A "thou shalt" or "thou shalt not" implies its
opposite; prohibition arises only in response to, to correct, an antithetical tendency, one always implying and
limiting the other. A scientist organizes opposition to
propositional assertions in the effort to validate or in-
validate them; he asserts, organizes counter-assertions,
plans experiments giving voice to the opposition, and
weighs evidence, checking each assertion against its
negation.

(The unfolding or development of action according to
entelechial implications or an entelechial principle of
order appears to bear some relation to the mechanical

solidarity of a social system—based on shared values, beliefs, and sentiments—characteristic according to Parsons of the pattern-maintenance and goal-attainment subsystems of a society. The unfolding or development of action according to admonitory implications or an admonitory principle of order appears to bear some relation to the organic solidarity of a social system—based on differentiated, complementary roles—characteristic according to Parsons of the adaptation and integration subsystems of a society.)

Burke, too, has a fourfold classification—in his work, it is a classification of primary linguistic dimensions or types of language: 1) logical or propositional; 2) poetic; 3) rhetorical; and 4) ethical. It is consistent with Burke's general position to regard each type of language as a mode of persuasion, which induces cooperation (solidarity) by creating a particular kind of shared symbolic world. Words do not essentially stand for concepts or forms of knowledge, but are rather hortatory acts of communion, creating shared sympathies, purposes, and basic orientations. (A word or statement is an *attitude,* "rephrased in accordance with the strategy of revision made necessary by the recalcitrance of the materials employed for embodying this attitude.")

A shared system of symbols is the necessary condition for cooperative action. Science uses propositional language. Art uses poetic language. History, which examines man's past to judge or sanction his actions, or law, which sanctions, uses rhetorical language. Religion uses ethical language. Each type of language, as a special mode of persuasion, locates or appeals to certain grounds, motives, or reasons for action.

Even closer to us, in the realm of mental illness, Harry Stack Sullivan in a paper in *Schizophrenia as a Human*

Process quotes Adolph Meyer as defining in 1907 the property of mental reactions (as a type of biological reaction) to be the occurrence of a system of symbolization. "From this viewpoint," writes Sullivan in 1925, "it will be seen that any problem in psychopathology becomes a problem of symbol functioning, a matter of seeking to understand and interpret eccentric symbol performances." Symbolization is as much a part of man's biology as the physiological processes that—from the point of view of the study of personality—constitute the conditions and resources for symbolic processes.

There is nothing mystical, although much is still mysterious, in this conception of man, which focuses on a unique capacity, appearing in a living organism that has achieved a certain degree of complexity and differentiation. The most casual inspection of man's actions would indicate that these are not dependent in any simple way upon his past or present experience. He continually, through symbolization, creates and recreates his past and acts in part at least in terms of his own imagination of it, rather than simply as it objectively "was" (even supposing that could be unequivocally determined). He is able, through symbolization, to imagine future states of affairs and expends effort to alter objective situations to conform to such imagined states of affairs.

Animals, including man, are able to respond to signals. Signals announce or indicate what is, has been, or will be present. Signals are intrinsic or arbitrary; that is, signals are a natural part of, or a convention attached to, the presence they announce or indicate. Man, however, certainly alone among all animals, is able to evoke, to remind himself, to anticipate that of which there is no sign at all. Man's symbolizations are independent of his immediate physical environment. A moment's reflection will convince you that this characteristic of his thought carries with it the potentiality for either unusual achievement or disaster; one can hardly avoid an ironic attitude toward this great gift.

Man symbolizes the invisible; only man is capable of appreciating the negative. He alone is able in the presence of "yes" to imagine "no," in the absence of "anything" to imagine "something," in the presence of "that which is" to imagine and act in terms of "that which is not," and in any situation to imagine alternatives and their possible consequences. His imagined world, the world created by the exercise of the symbolizing function, is not a simple replication, summation, or extract of experience with objective situations, but is rather a novel invention, which is imposed upon the objective situation and determines its meaning and therefore action in relation to it.

Man, in this view of him, lives in a world of value as well as a world of fact. Note that rationality, which concerns means-ends relations, is irrelevant to the problem of choosing between ultimate ends or values. There is no instrumental reason or purely cognitive standard for preferring one ultimate end or value over another. The achievement of such ends in action, however, is limited by the availability of objective means and by the extent of man's willingness to expend effort to master means and to overcome objective obstacles.

Man is neither a creature of conditions nor a passive embodiment or manifestation of transcendental ideas that live through him. Man makes choices or expresses preferences between alternatives. He accounts for such choices by reference to "motives," "feelings," "ideas" (nonscientific as well as scientific ideas), which are represented by symbols. Man is active, not reactive. He creates a world of meaning in terms of which he acts. He does not respond to things as they are, but to the meaning things have for him. These meanings may be inferred from his actions or represented by him in symbols. Man does not simply react to stimuli, but makes an effort to realize in action—through mastering means and overcoming obstacles—patterns or states of affairs conceived by him and deemed by him to be desirable. That is to say, man acts in a world of symbolic conceptions. He is oriented to imagined states of affairs, conceptions of the future. He is motivated by commitments to realize (or avoid) such states of affairs through action. Man's creative activity depends upon the symbolization function and cannot be understood without reference to a subjective frame of reference—that is, how things seem or are conceived or represented, what states of affairs are imagined and function as ends or goals, in the mind of man.

You may well ask here, why the formulation that man *chooses* between alternatives in assigning meaning to any situation in which he acts? Why is the meaning of the situation not determined a priori by the objective characteristics of his environment and hereditary endowment? Talcott Parsons especially has emphasized that man must be conceived as choosing between alternatives because of the ambiguity of the object world and the plasticity of the nervous system. The significance of a situation to a man is not predetermined by intrinsic characteristics of that situation or anything in it. Man's genetically determined constitution does not automatically determine, over a very wide range, his intentions in a particular situation.

The necessity of interpretation implies alternative frameworks of meaning, within each of which occurs a particular kind of symbolization. I have already shown you how examples of such frameworks of meaning, as these are given primacy in various types of action or highly differentiated works of man, are to be found in the work of Burke, Cassirer, Freud, and Parsons. First, there is the adaptive frame of reference exemplified in instrumental action and ego functioning, and by science. Instrumental action, ego functioning, and science are concerned with the relation of means to ends, and give primacy to cognitive standards of truth, validity, or efficiency. Second, there is the expressive frame of reference exemplified in expressive action and id processes, and by art. Expressive action, id processes, and art represent meanings by expressive symbolizations—emotions may be regarded as such expressive symbolizations—and give primacy to appreciative or aesthetic standards of appropriateness, taste, or beauty. The moral frame of reference is exemplified in responsible action and superego functioning, and by law. Responsible action, superego functioning, and law are concerned with moral evaluations in terms of systems of norms and give primacy to integrative standards of right and wrong. Finally, the value frame of reference is exemplified in commitments to patterns of ideals, values, and beliefs, in ego-ideal processes, and by religion. Value-commitments, ego-ideal processes, and religion maintain patterns of beliefs about nonempirical aspects of reality and ultimate value-orientations.

I should like to reemphasize here that while "real" external reality may be presumed to exist independently of its apprehension, it cannot be known except symbolically—as part, then, of psychic reality insofar as psychic reality is constituted by symbolic processes. Even the experience of simple sensations involves interpretation in a framework of meaning. Science does not involve

direct knowledge of "real" reality but an interpretation
of reality in a particular framework of meaning. The
achievement of science is its system of highly abstract
cognitive representations of reality, to a great extent
freed of particular sensuous connotations. However, science among the works of man does not offer or lead to
the only or necessarily the best interpretation of reality
for all purposes or requirements of an individual or
group. The utility of science or an adaptive-cognitive
orientation to reality for the adaptive mastery of reality
has tended to lead to their overvaluation in the behavioral sciences and to a concomitant lack of appreciation
of other works of man and other orientations to reality
as involving meaningful, functional frameworks of
meaning within which one may orient to and represent
reality. Heinz Hartmann has made a similar point
throughout his writings in suggesting that rational action
is not the only or always the best means of achieving an
optimal relation between man and his environment.

Man is not pushed by a chaos of wants, but drawn by
ends of his own imagining, which are related to one
another in more or less integrated systems of symbolized meanings. Such systems may be studied, and they
are important to study. A set of personal or internalized
symbolic systems and the relations between these different symbolic systems constitute the personality system.
(I may add here that the emergent or distinctive property of a social system is the existence of a common,
more or less integrated, system of symbolized meanings
shared by its members.)

Since man's actions are a resultant of the interdependent interaction of subjective and objective elements,
and since a variety of symbolic systems are possible
among which man may choose, man must have a variety

of histories, his social life is inevitably to some extent pluralistic, and evolution is neither necessarily linear nor progressive.

Parsons' theory of action in sociology and the theory of psychoanalysis of Freud converge in this view of man. In fact, I believe that Freud would receive greater credit as its architect if his positivistic assumptions had not interfered with his own realization that his discoveries cried out for a conceptual frame of reference appropriate to such a view of man. But that is a lot to expect of a great innovator—that he question the very certainties he stands upon and from which he is able to impel himself into the future toward a creation whose final form he himself is doomed, like Moses, never to see.

As it is, incredible, perplexing, even humorous strains are evident in Freud's writing. He longs for eventual rapprochement with neurophysiology, while he analyzes the meaning of a dream. He utilizes a reflex reduction of tension model replete with references to external and internal stimuli, while discovering patterns in the linguistic productions of patients and—would such a discovery be possible for anyone but a rationalist?—the nature of a thought process operating according to principles entirely different from ordinary rational thought. He is preoccupied with displacements and transformations of energy, while he develops a tool of investigation and treatment that relies solely on understanding verbal transactions occurring under carefully controlled conditions. He thinks of instinct and of libidinal phases, while he observes the ubiquity of certain groups of metaphors he terms oral, anal, and phallic, and the penetration of any one of these in verbal and nonverbal symbolic transformations into every crevice of a patient's experience of himself and reality and the very nature of the ends the patient seeks. He apologizes for the fact that his case studies read rather like the products of the novelist's art than the scientist's sober investigations, and at the same time discovers that memory and phantasy have effects as striking as any nonsubjective constitutional or situational variable. Heredity and early life experience he holds to be important aspects of his frame of reference, although his method denies him any possibility for the direct investigation of either, and an apocryphal tale has him replying sublimely to an objection to his report of a patient's experience with a psychoanalyst in the center of England—the objection being that, in fact, there was not and never had been a psychoanalyst in that vicinity—that "If the patient says a psychoanalyst is there, then there is a psychoanalyst there."

I think you may agree with me that Freud's courage, his ability to transcend his own conceptual predilections, are truly astonishing. Despite his positivist belief that psychological phenomena would eventually be completely explained by neurophysiology, a belief that perhaps as a man of his own time he never completely abandoned, he was nevertheless bold enough to abandon a strategy founded on that belief. At a crucial point in his career, he decided to study psychological phenomena as if these constituted an empirical realm in their own right for the explanation of which a conceptual system couched in psychological language was required. He thereby discovered a realm of symbolic processes, which he called "psychic reality." This psychic reality included the inner world of phantasies, conscious and unconscious, imagined states of affairs deemed desirable and toward the realization of which action could be understood to be oriented.

That patients suffer from "reminiscences" was an

early formulation of Freud's giving primacy to symbolic process in etiology. This insight of his was considerably enriched by his fortunate and dramatic recovery from his "mistake" in ascribing causal status to supposed actual, objective, sexual seductions in childhood in accounting for neurotic illness. He saw instead that "mere" phantasies of relationships, phantasies of events —symbolizations of a special kind—may also have causal efficacy.

In discovering transference, he discovered that an objectively existent social being, the physician, for example, and relationships with such objective beings, may serve as symbolic representations or recreations of past experience.

The dominant theme in Freud's empirical work is a view of man in terms of conflicting motives as these are manifested in symbolic processes with different characteristics and aims. The concepts of conscious and unconscious, of ego, superego, and id, may be regarded, in part at least, as classifications of types of symbolizations, regulated in different ways and with reference to different kinds of ends or goals. Internal conflict between tendencies, and the symptoms which represent compromises between different tendencies, likewise may be understood in terms of the interaction and mutual influence of different kinds of symbolizations. The concept "superego" most clearly, perhaps, refers to a symbolic invention. It does not arise in any simple way from either experience or what is genetically given alone. Once in existence, as part of the personality system, it accounts for man's actions as a third relatively independent variable, together with representations both of current experience and physiological processes.

Freud's discovery and description of two modes of

symbolization—primary and secondary process—will probably survive as one of his greatest achievements. It is important to emphasize now, in preparation for a later discussion of mental illness (and of schizophrenia as an illustration of mental illness) that primary process thinking should not be regarded as a debasement of rational or secondary process thinking, but as an independent form of thinking which in its own right may contribute to important achievements. With regard to the achievement of such criteria as survival, creativity, understanding, expressiveness, adaptation, or health, both secondary and primary process thinking may contribute either functionally or dysfunctionally. Primary process thinking in and of itself cannot be pathognomonic of mental illness.

From the discovery that patients suffer from reminiscences, that is, from symbolizations of the past, and then that these reminiscences are not true representations of the past but phantasy, you should not conclude that mental illness is equivalent to subjugation to phantasy, to the nonrational, while mental health is equivalent to recognition of brute reality. This in effect equates health with cognitive-rational symbolization and denies any but dysfunctional effects to other modes of symbolization. Furthermore, the assumption underlying the notion that so-called reality confrontation is an antidote to phantasy is: there is one true reality; it is possible to know it directly, independently of any imaginative apprehension or valuation of it. But it would seem instead that all knowledge of reality is symbolically mediated. Reality is always a symbolic creation. Different modes of symbolization are functional or dysfunctional with respect to particular goals or interests in relation to which they are employed. In simple terms, if you want to write a poem, make a scientific discovery, or choose a wife, primary process thinking may be exceptionally valuable; if you want to hammer a nail, it can be a damned nuisance.

Freud described primary process thinking in terms of such characteristics as condensation and displacement as well as the absence of conformity to the categories and rules of logic. (Note, following Kenneth Burke, that processes like condensation and displacement are probably particular aspects or resources of any symbolic system or language. Abstraction involves something similar to condensation; displacement is clearly related to metaphor.) Because schizophrenia especially among the mental illnesses has been described as involving an impairment of the capacity to abstract as well as a relative domination of primary process thinking, I might just as well state here that I think it is possible that primary process thinking may in fact best be understood as a type of abstraction.

Briefly, secondary process thinking may involve essentially abstraction by extension, which includes both differentiation and generalization. Through abstraction by extension, a concrete entity or event becomes a particular case of a more general law, idea, class, or series. The meaning of any experience is extended by relating it to other experiences; through such extension, any entity or event is experienced in a context, a series or order in which it has location, a law of which it is a particular example, a class of which it is a member. Abstraction by extension creates the bonds connecting, comparing, and systematically combining entities or events. Yet each entity or event, even as its meaning expands, even as its implications are explicated, retains its distinct identity and limitation; even as it fits into a universe, it remains independent and singular.

Interestingly enough, there seems to be a similarity between reality as conceived through abstraction by extension and the organic solidarity of a social community in which each individuated part makes its unique, differentiated, necessary contribution to the achievement of a shared end. May we expect that abstraction by extension is the important process of symbolization in those subsystems of society characterized by organic solidarity—that is, in the adaptation and integration subsystems of a social system the outputs of which are, respectively, instrumental action and responsible action? Abstraction by extension does seem to be the process by which symbols are generated in science and history, cultural systems relevant to the adaptation and integration subsystems of the social system.

Primary process thinking, on the other hand, may involve essentially abstraction by intension. The concentration and separate characterization of abstraction by intension contrast with the expansion and universalization of abstraction by extension. Abstraction by intension acts to separate an entity or event from any context at all, thereby embedding it in shadow, endowing it with mystery, or surrounding it with an aura of special quality. Abstraction by intension isolates an undifferentiated totality, an essence, out of which characters may emerge. These characters, however, do not possess any individuality apart from the whole from which they emerge; they do not simply "stand for" that whole, but are identical with it, possessors of its entire value. Abstraction by intension focuses on an entity or event as an immediate presence having no context; therefore such an entity or event has no past and no future, is comparable to, tempered by, related to, or mitigated by nothing else, and as immediate presence commands total attention or fills consciousness. Abstraction by intension results in an intensification of the entity or event or, perhaps more exactly, of whatever value it has. Much is compressed in such an entity or event; any entities or events which share its value are absorbed by it; there is a condensation of all such entities or events. Such concentration, intensification, telescoping, compression, syncretic fusion, such violently separate characterization, such immediacy and totality, permitting no quantitative distinctions, extinguishing all differences—so that every part of the whole is identical with the whole and contains its entire significance, value, or potency— are, of course, recognizable as characteristic of primary process thinking as well as, as we have previously noted, what Ernst Cassirer has described in similar terms as mythic thinking. What perhaps is not so generally realized is that this kind of thinking is not nonabstract (which would mean asymbolic) but is in fact a special type of abstraction transforming experience through definable operations that create certain conceptions of experience and call for special symbols to represent these conceptions.

You have heard that man has been conceived as acting under the influence of blindly impelling instincts. Freud's concept of instincts is often misunderstood as denoting the operation of physiological processes. He quite clearly meant by "instinct" the psychic representatives of physiological processes and by "id" an organization of such psychic representatives. By psychic representatives he clearly meant a particular kind of symbolization. You should consider that if a man under the influence of primary process thinking behaves as if he is irresistibly compelled, preoccupied, or awed, it is not necessary to account for such effects by recourse to hypothetical drives or instincts. The compulsion exerted by such conceptions may follow from the nature of the mode of symbolization from which they spring.

Again, we may take a moment to notice that the "community of essence" conceived through abstraction by intension is similar to the mechanical solidarity of a homogenous social community in which the members share similar values, beliefs, and sentiments, in which involvement rather than individuation is required of these members. One might expect that abstraction by intension is the important process of symbolization in those subsystems of society characterized by mechanical solidarity—that is, the goal-attainment and pattern-maintenance subsystems of a social system the outputs of which are, respectively, expressive action and (to the system itself) the maintenance and generation of value-commitments. Abstraction by intension does seem to be the process by which symbols are generated in art and religion, cultural systems relevant to the goal-attainment and pattern-maintenance subsystems of the social system.

What does this view of man imply for our idea of mental illness and the body of knowledge germane to the treatment of mental illness?

Symbolization may go awry or be impaired. Disorders of integration and adaptation result from such impairment. Psychiatry, as one of the healing arts, may be regarded as the treatment—often, by no means exclusively, but perhaps most significantly, through symbolic means—of impairments of symbolization. Such impairments of symbolization usually (but, given the limiting cases, not always) have origins, or are aggravated by processes, in all four systems of interest to the psychiatrist—the physiological behavioral system, the personality system, the social system, and the cultural system —and the complicated relationships among them. It is often difficult to know, with respect to a particular impairment of symbolization, to what system or relationship between systems treatment should be directed.

What is the basic-science knowledge applied in psychiatry? In my view, it is the body of knowledge concerned with man's symbolizing activities and achievements. More particularly, it is knowledge about the conditions of, and resources for, symbolic processes in the physiological behavioral system. It is knowledge about the symbolization of motivational dispositions and their fates in the personality system. It is knowledge about the interaction of entities according to shared patterns of meaning in the social system. It is knowledge about the characteristics of cultural systems—organizations of symbolic entities or works of man, such as language, myth, science, art, law, and religion, which may be institutionalized in social systems and internalized in personality systems.

But more about the idea of a mental illness when next we meet.

2: The Idea of a Mental Illness

Ladies and gentlemen:

The last time we met I tried to convince you of the importance of man's symbolizing activities. Following our meeting, one of you scolded me for my complacent arrogance in claiming that man's capacity to symbolize was unique among animals—that symbolization had arisen as a new, an emergent, biological function only at the level of complexity and differentiation characteristic of him. I stand my ground. Moreover, I am moved to comment that it is especially necessary for physicians, who so often must look at man from the viewpoint of the anus, to remember that it is this same man, who, miraculously, also speaks—also creates language.

Our patient does not simply die. He knows that he dies. He imagines it. He may speak of it. As physicians, we are as much involved with his knowledge, his anticipation, his conceptions of death as with the fact of death itself. I hope that you will think twice before joining the ranks of those whose thinking begins "Man is nothing but . . ." or whose response to any of man's achievements is "That is nothing but . . ." followed by references to animal ancestors or to the mouth, anus, and genitals. As physicians we may not turn away from either the high or the low, if we are to know man truly and to care for him.

Now I become somewhat embarrassed by my inclination to digress, and I willingly allow myself to be led by your impatience back to our subject.

What is a disease? I commend to you an answer to that question I once received from a student who somewhat hesitantly said to me, "There is no such thing as a disease." The important word is "thing." Too often in medicine we reify diseases, whether tuberculosis, infantile paralysis, or schizophrenia, as if they were tangible entities to be finally discovered and directly observed some day. I probably do not need to remind you that as physicians we observe only signs and symptoms and only particular instances of these. The disease itself—any disease, I am not just talking about psychiatric disease—is a *concept,* some ideal type we have in our minds (as physicians, we too are deeply involved with symbolization). We refer to this symbolic representation or ideal type whenever we encounter a particular instance to see to what extent instance and concept match. Some investigators (Charcot, for example, in studying hysteria), confusing concept and instance, recommend studying the most extreme forms of a disease, as if the exaggeration of clinical features will reveal the "true" disease to us.

Disease is necessarily a "historical" concept; that is, any disease represents an imagined sequence of events. Signs and symptoms are the objectively observable manifestations of an inferred process. (Do you think it would be correct to say that signs are interpreted by us to signify that a particular kind of event or moment in a sequence has occurred or is occurring, while symptoms are the patient's symbolic representations of his conception of what has occurred or is occurring?)

One class of events is made up of those events that are termed etiologic. Etiologic events are those that are necessary and those that are sufficient to initiate the inferred disease process.

The relations among etiologic events are quite complicated. A necessary event may occur without initiating the disease process if other events that must occur with it or in some relation to it—perhaps even in a certain order—for such initiation to take place are absent. Events that are sufficient in the presence of a necessary event to initiate the disease process may in the absence of the necessary event have no such effect.

Certainly in part because of the way we think, we find that we conceive etiologic events to be located some place—in the situation of the system or in a part or parts of the system itself. For example, as far as the personality system itself is concerned, an etiologic event may occur in its situation. That is, it may occur in the physiological behavioral organism, a system of physico-chemical entities which conceptually must be regarded as outside of or an aspect of the situation of the personality system. The etiologic event may also occur in the physical or social environment of the personality system. On the other hand, an etiologic event may be thought to arise in a part or parts of the system itself. So, in the personality system, motivational dispositions or tendencies (or, more properly, the symbolization of such dispositions or tendencies), or a combination of kinds of dispositions or tendencies (again, more properly, a combination of kinds of symbolizations), occur that are held to be necessary, sufficient, or both, to initiate dysfunctional consequences for the personality system.

Etiologic events occurring in the situation of the system initiate a dysfunctional or disease process by altering the availability of means, resources, or capacities required by the system if functions are to be performed, ends achieved, or goals attained. Etiologic events occurring in a part or parts of the system initiate a dysfunctional or disease process by altering internal arrangements between parts of the system required by the system if functions are to be performed, ends achieved, or goals attained.

I remind you now that such distinctions between systems and between a system and its situation are theoretical and the location of events according to such a schema, while no doubt heuristic and perhaps the only way we can think about these matters, is also theoretical. I beg you not to ask me if personality systems and physiological behavioral organisms are "really" distinct, existent entities—I never expect to see either one, any more than I expect to see a disease—or whether an etiologic event actually occurs in a personality system or in a physiological behavioral organism. Although an organism probably seems real to you and a personality system fictive, I assure you that both are abstractions and neither is a thing or a place.

It is important to remember that when focus is upon the personality system and, therefore, upon symbolic processes an etiologic event may be the occurrence of a symbolic representation and not an actual event. Piaget has stated that the purposive, compensating activities of a psychological system are, frequently, a response to virtual intrusions rather than actual intrusions. That is, because man symbolizes, he anticipates future states of affairs; he is able to imagine the possibility of inimical states of affairs; he responds to his symbolic representations of such states of affairs with purposive activities meant to compensate for such disturbances in advance of their actual occurrence. Since man is above all a symbolizing animal, such symbolized or virtual intrusions and the compensatory activities in response to them, which may have significant dysfunctional consequences, constitute an important kind of disease process.

A radical view of psychological disease or mental ill-

ness is that the etiologic event is always symbolic: symbolizations, anticipated or virtual intrusions, pathogenic
phantasies, psychic reality. The human misery that is
simply—that is, with no significant dependence upon
symbolic mediation—a coerced response to actual environmental or organic intrusion would not be regarded as
psychological or mental illness. Such a view follows
from the effort to remain consistently within the conceptual framework of the personality system. Since,
however, human behavior is almost always to some extent symbolically determined, one probably must conceive a continuum involving varying proportions of symbolic and nonsymbolic etiologic events. Our interest,
insofar as we examine human behavior from the point
of view of the personality system, is concentrated upon
the symbolically dominated end of that continuum.

A second class of events in the disease process is made
up of the altered states of the system said to be diseased. These events are thought to follow, to be responses to, etiologic events. As suggested by the previous discussion, these altered states are dysfunctional.
They are states of malintegration or states of maladapta-
tion or (usually) both. That is, they are states in which
the arrangements or relations between parts of the system have departed from some optimal state, or states in
which the relation of the system and its environment
has departed from some optimal state, or (usually) both.
One may further distinguish, on the one hand, responses
to the etiologic event that represent departures from
optimal states—perhaps one such departure in a system
of interdependent entities leading to still another kind
or degree of departure from the optimal and that to still
another. On the other hand, some responses represent
tendencies in the system to return to an optimal state.

The aim is reparative or restitutional, though the actual as distinct from the intended consequences of the action of such a tendency may be either functional or dysfunctional. In this connection, I remind you of the reparative scarring tendency set into motion by a wound that nevertheless may result in the dysfunctional keloid.

A third class of events includes the system's response to the responses, sometimes inimical, of others (some of these others are physicians) to the diseased state. The system's response to such interventions by others may, again, be a further or different kind of departure from an optimal state or a compensatory effort to prevent such a departure; that effort also may have functional or dysfunctional consequences.

A fourth class of events includes the more or less permanent end-states of the disease process conceived to be possible, likely, or inevitable, along with some notion of the kind of events that are thought to influence the possibility, likelihood, or inevitability of various end-states.

To understand a disease, then, is to have a concept of a process or sequence of events and a theory with verifiable implications that correlates particular signs and symptoms with particular classes of inferred events. A transient sign or symptom is ordinarily not considered a manifestation of disease unless the inference is made, and verifiable, that such a sign or symptom has significance in terms of a sequence of events, a disease process in time, however long or short. One may make the inference that a disease continues silently, exists in latent form, or is in remission during periods free of signs or symptoms. Different conceptions of a particular mental illness (for example, schizophrenia) may attribute different meanings to a given sign or symptom with respect to the inferred disease process. Thus, a particular sign or symptom may be regarded by different investigators as evidence, for example, of the destructive effects of an etiologic event, an effort at compensation or repair by the affected system, or an end-state.

Incidentally, you will recognize that the concept of disease involves an equilibrium model. It is hard to think about any aspect of man without recourse to such a model. In varying forms, it is central, for example, in psychoanalytic theory, Parsons' theory of action, Cannon's formulations about homeostasis, and Bertalannffy's general system theory.

Let us agree, then, that mental illness, like any disease, is first of all a concept or idea—and that, therefore, any particular mental illness such as schizophrenia is also a concept or idea. Do you agree also that it may prove useful to distinguish mental illness from other diseases as involving primarily an impairment of symbolic functioning? My guess is that you prefer that formulation to the more radical one—that the concept mental illness necessarily includes the idea of an illness that is the effect of symbolic events or virtual intrusions, of internalized representations of self or the object world. This more radical formulation holds that the etiologic event of mental illness, the event to which the illness is a response, is always located in psychic reality, is always ultimately an internalized, relatively stable or structuralized symbolic form or forms representing a conception or conceptions of reality—and never events in the situation (whether physiological organism or external reality) in and of themselves.

If you draw back from this formulation, I don't wonder at that. You are quick to sense that a possible implication of such a formulation might be that no amount of alteration of the situation (whether physiological organism or social system) will radically *cure* a mental illness so defined, *once it has come into being*—that is, once an internalized symbolic structure effects and maintains it. Such an implication cannot be easily accepted in these times when so much human misery, so obviously a response to the physical and social conditions of human life, commands our attention and demands of us alleviation. Perhaps we can avoid such an unhappy conclusion. We shall see.

It is, of course, possible to study a mental illness in terms of neurophysiological structures and processes, which, strictly speaking, must be considered the conditions for, and the determinants of the availability of resources limiting, symbolic functioning. It is possible to study a mental illness as a manifestation of systems of internalized symbolizations, regulated according to different principles and with different aims or tendencies, constituting the personality system. It is possible to study a mental illness as a manifestation of the characteristics of a system of interaction such as a family, community, or society, which is constituted by the symbol systems its members share. It is also possible to study a mental illness from the point of view of a cultural system of beliefs and values, which, when institutionalized in social systems or internalized in personality systems, govern beliefs about and attitudes toward mental illness.

It should be clear that I do not believe that any one of these approaches to the study of any mental illness has the right, conceptually speaking, to first claim upon scientific interest or to scientific validity. It is, however, useful for consistency of focus and conceptual clarity to distinguish between them.

But, following now our own interest in these lectures, we may ask: how in fact do psychiatrists study the personality system—and a mental illness such as schizophrenia from the point of view of the personality system? Not that there is a one-to-one relation between an investigator's method of study and his conception of a particular mental illness. Not at all. A conception may lead to a preference for a method of study and a method of study may influence the formation of a conception. Method and idea influence each other in a complicated way in the history of science, the invention of methods leading to new ideas, and ideas, no matter how vague, determining how and at what we look.

Suppose you wanted to discover something about a mental illness—again, let us stick to our example, schizophrenia—or you had some ideas about it you wanted to test. How might you begin?

Most simply perhaps you might, as Bleuler did, examine a large number of patients, asking questions, studying their verbal, affective, and motoric products, observing their performances as each attempts to solve some standard problem you set. You end up with a list of cardinal or primary features, which, you hope, distinguish this class of patients from any other, and another list of secondary features, which may or may not be present in such patients. But these secondary features, even when present, do not distinguish these patients from those belonging to some other class. You decide that the illness in some patients has an insidious onset, because there is no apparent triggering event, and that in others the onset has more discernible cause. You conjecture that the former patients suffer from an organic defect of some sort, since you can discover nothing else to account for their malady.

Ladies and gentlemen, I am sorry to be disagreeable, but I must argue with your results. You have already forgotten that it is the *animal symbolicum* that we study. If the symbolization function operates, then behavior is not our datum, but rather the meanings of behavior. If I ask you what is the meaning of the behavior of a man falling from the third floor to the first floor, you quite rightly respond that that question is meaningless. This man's fall follows the laws of Newton; so would any other man's fall. He is a physical thing. You have no objection to my assigning him to the class of physical things. But if I ask you what is the meaning of the behavior of a man who jumps out of the third floor window, you immediately understand that here is a different situation. The behavior of the man who jumps—assuming he is not coerced to do so; if he is pushed he behaves as any other physical thing—depends on the intention, whether conscious or not, with which he jumps, on the nature of his symbolizations of past and present experience and his anticipations of the future—yes, at that moment he imagines the future. You cannot answer the question concerning the meaning of his behavior merely by observing the behavior, no matter how meticulously or with what refinements of quantification you do so. You would certainly caution me about putting the man who jumps in the same class as all other men who jump and labelling this class the jumping disease. Quite rightly, you see that the behavior may be a final common pathway for a number of quite different processes. You would, I think, not advise me to attempt to discover the nature of these processes by taking motion pictures of men jumping, and separating those who jump rapidly from those who are hesitant, those who leap from those who crouch, those who cry from those who are silent.

Insofar, then, as we view phenomena from the point of view of the personality system, that is, from the point of view of internalized systems of symbolization with different characteristics and aims, no observable behavior always has the same meaning, whether one man repeats it or it is observed of many men, any more than a word always has the same meaning when spoken by many different men or on different occasions by the same man'. Furthermore, the probability is great that any behavior on any occasion has at the same time more than one meaning, just as any word is a nidus of intersecting meanings, is surrounded by a nimbus of meanings belonging to different levels of organization of symbolization. Language is intrinsically ambiguous, and so is human behavior. Using positivistic terms, we speak in psychoanalysis of the multiple determination of any phenomenon in psychology, but you will recognize that causation is not at issue here but rather a characteristic of phenomena involving symbolization.

If I guess rightly, you now seem ready to complain that if no behavior always has the same meaning and every behavior has many meanings, it is impossible to study man scientifically. I agree even before you say so that the study of man is marvelously difficult.

Nevertheless, I cannot disregard, even to make things easier, the possibility that your conclusion that an insidious onset is apparently without adequate cause, your description that affect is inappropriate or associations loose or disorganized, tell me more about you than about the patient. Your conclusions and descriptions tell me that you cannot make sense of the patient, but do not convince me that the patient does not make sense. The confidence of your assertions is based on your assumption that what is meaningless to you has no meaning to the patient. We have here a defect in our investigating instrument, which we should not confuse with the defect we hope to investigate. In other words, "insidious onset" means you did not understand the etiology of the illness; "inappropriate affect" means you did not know what symbolization of events motivated the affect or lack of it or its connection with certain contents; "disorganized associations" means associations you could not follow.

For these dubious results, I blame your method, which involves wresting samples of behavior from their context, which you ignore, and treating such behaviors as primary data in and of themselves. You ignore the nature of the clinical setting in which you examine the patient; you ignore what that setting means to him, what being tested in that setting means to him, and what you mean to him. Therefore, if the patient should be attempting to create and communicate a symbolic representation of his experience—with whatever re-sources he has at his command, including his inappro-priate affect and his loose associations, and with an organization in part determined by the nature of those resources—the likelihood is great that such an effort will communicate nothing to you.

Incidentally, in science allusion to residual factors as causative (such as, in this case, "organic" or "constitu-tional")—that is, factors outside the conceptual frame of reference chosen—is always a confession of ignorance. Perhaps, too often, it is also a flight from more cogent inquiry within that frame of reference.

I warn you that I will probably make similar objec-tions if you want to do statistical studies of the appearance of this or that behavioral datum in groups of patients. I cannot, for example, make myself believe that one can assume the same behavior in any patient or in the same patient on different occasions checked off on a rating list always means aggression, dependency, regression, or what have you, because it looks aggressive, dependent, or regressive to an observer. Such studies may purport to test psychoanalytic hypotheses, for example, involving such notions as aggression, dependency, or regression; I cannot accept their claims to do so adequately.

Perhaps I have convinced some of you that the methods of clinical observation of sample performances and of statistical correlations of behavioral items may either bias us in the direction of attributing meaninglessness to phenomena or coarsely blunt and blur the meanings and the differences in meaning of what we observe. Feeling discouraged, you are now inclined to abandon classification and hypotheses altogether. If I insist on introducing the symbolization function, you will insist that scientific explanation is impossible, even that the idealistic conception of unique and irreducibly individual man steadily grows more to your liking in dealing with psychological matters. You prefer to abandon the attempt to understand a particular mental illness and attempt instead by talking to an individual person, by listening carefully to his own accounts of his illness, by grasping intuitively what it has meant to him in his own terms, only to understand that person, with no pretense at generalization, theory, or explanation. You may even begin using words like existential psychology, phenomenology, encounter, and I will then become somewhat frightened and withdraw in haste because neither as physician or scientist do I know how to respond to these ideas.

On the whole, though, I commend your intention to begin by listening carefully to what a patient has to say about his experience. I am afraid, nevertheless, that being an *animal symbolicum* yourself you will not be able to avoid having certain preconceptions or developing certain conceptions of what ails your patient. I do not advise you to try to maintain a kind of conceptual innocence or nudity, in the vain hope that such an effort will enable you to grasp experience immediately in and of itself. If you are determined not to theorize, you will simply end up theorizing poorly or naively without being aware that you have done so, or you may uncritically adopt the patient's theories about what is going on inside him. These theories, which like all scientific theory are full of metaphor, even when they involve reference to demons or a demoniacal reality, to quantities of some stuff or other that flows here and there, to inner boilers about to burst, have a great deal of interest for us, so much so and so much may we find ourselves in agreement with them, that we may forget to inquire how it is that the patient forms these particular theories about himself, entertains these particular phantasies, symbolizes in just this way and not in some other. Since the patient tends to take his symbolizations for granted, he is not usually of immediate help in answering this kind of question.

Conceptions of a mental illness such as schizophrenia often involve postulation of certain events in early infancy. I myself am somewhat leery of analogies between the symbolizations of adult schizophrenic patients and those of childhood based on the fact that the former appear to us to be in some ways primitive or regressed. By regressed we usually mean not organized according to the usual adult model of waking consciousness. However, as Freud pointed out, regression in this formal sense is not the same as regression in a temporal sense; that is, regression from one state to another, from one level of organization to another, is not the same as regression backward in time. It is only because we are so persistently sequential in our thinking, and so preoccupied with explanation by antecedents or historical origin, that we leap instantly and unreflectingly from formal regression to temporal regression. Adult schizophrenic persons are not big children, and my experience with children has not led me to the conclusion that the schizophrenic person has simply returned to a form of symbolization he knew as a child, or that children symbolize the way schizophrenic persons do.

However, you, as others do, may wish to contribute to our study of a mental illness such as schizophrenia by making direct observations of children and infants, including, where possible, the sophisticated longitudinal study. I have some cautions before you begin, in addition to those I have already expressed about the observation of behavior divorced from considerations of its meaning, consideration of meaning being rendered difficult here by the relative sparseness of the child's resources for communication. Remember that you are inclined to see things in rather simple cause and effect sequences and to impose continuity on your observations, to see one thing leading to another in a series of tiny, hardly separable steps. In this connection I was recently reminded by one of my teachers (William Pious) of the furor caused by the idea of quantum jumps in physics. Yet it seems possible that there are discontinuous jumps in development (as well as from one psychological state to another), and that what went before bears little resemblance to and cannot be said to be the cause of what came after. The appearance of symbolic thought in infancy is, I believe, such a discontinuity. An infant incapable of symbolization—and I am not, you realize, speaking of recognition of and response to signals—and an infant capable of it, no matter in what rudimentary form, seem worlds apart to me, their behavior as far different and requiring as much change in the conceptual frame of reference within which it is regarded as the behavior of the thing-man falling freely through space and that of the *animal symbolicum* jumping out a window. The reasoning of those who like Susan Isaacs justify extrapolations from the verbal communications of an older child to the meaning of the play of a younger one and from the inferred symbolic meaning of such play to the phantasy life of an infant at the breast replete with symbolizations with different aims— because phenomena "must" be conceived in terms of a continuous series—ought, it seems to me, to be subjected to considerable qualification.

Along the same line, something observed at one point in an infant's or child's life should not be assumed to be a precursor of something more complicated at a later point, one thing leading inevitably to the other—a type of play, for example, leading to a later defense mechanism, or a kind of verbalization to a later complicated system of symbolizations. Things human being as complicated as they are, almost any event involving symbolization processes can probably be regarded as no more than a set of multiple potentialities the realization of which will depend upon other, unknown, unpredictable events, some of which will be nonsymbolic in character.

As symbol systems increase in complexity and differentiation, new capacities emerge that are not simple exten-
sions of previous ones and these serve new aims. (Heinz
Hartmann repeatedly pointed out that the function of a
particular psychological formation in the here-and-now
cannot be explained or derived simply by referring to its
supposed origin. As we have seen, Cassirer made a similar point in a different context.)

Finally, you may be interested in psychotherapy as a
method of generating and testing ideas about mental
illness. Psychotherapy is a method for studying symbolization processes and impairments of symbolization, and
for treating such impairments by symbolic means. Psychotherapy is a method of investigation to the extent
that it involves control of the conditions in which the
vicissitudes of symbolization are to be observed and in
which aspects of symbolization emerge that under other
conditions are not readily observed. There are, of
course, forms of psychotherapy in which there is little
attempt by the psychotherapist to control conditions in
the interest of minimal interference with the emergence
of the patient's symbolizations. There are forms of psychotherapy in which there is in fact little interest in
symbolic processes—rather an effort to alter what are
believed to be the effects of error and ignorance in the
patient's recognition of and response to verbal and other
signals.

Psychoanalysis is the most sophisticated form of psychotherapy, if the criteria are the extent to which skill is
brought to bear to control conditions in the interest of
minimal interference with the emergence of many kinds
of symbolization and the extent to which interest is
concentrated upon the symbolization function and not
upon other aspects of human behavior. (It follows from

this and previous formulations that I am somewhat skeptical that the findings of psychoanalysis or the conceptual framework relevant to its findings are sufficient to construct a general theory of human behavior. I do believe that in its realm in skillful hands it has no real peer at present as a theory of symbolization processes or as a method for investigating such processes.)

In the conditions maintained by a skillful psychoanalyst, a novel phenomenon, the transference neurosis, emerges; ideally the patient uses every detail of these carefully controlled conditions—his position vis-à-vis the analyst, the limits of time, fee transactions, the absence of conventional responses or usual cues, the opportunity for free association, the very silence—as media with which to create, shape, reveal symbolic representations of the unique reality in which he lives.

The transference neurosis is one of Freud's greatest scientific discoveries. Here is a phenomenon that is, to judge by complaints about the behavioral sciences, rare indeed in their realm. It is unexpected. It is of critical theoretical significance. It is replicable, under carefully controlled conditions.

The carefully controlled conditions are comprised by the psychoanalytic situation, which includes a patient capable of prolonged commitment to attempts at free association and a psychoanalyst whose participation is rigorously disciplined. The patient is willing and able to devote himself to making verbal productions in a situation designed to minimize *external* excitants, guidance, or interference that might evoke, shape, or obstruct these productions. Furthermore, he agrees himself to try to refrain from preventing in any way—as a result, for example, of deliberate efforts to order, select, or judge material—the utterance in verbal form of whatever comes to his mind. The psychoanalyst's aims in relation to the patient's verbal productions are limited to the interpretation of their meaning and the communication of such interpretations in a way that increases the likelihood that they will be meaningful to the patient; all the psychoanalyst's skills are exercised to these ends alone. Ideally, the psychoanalyst will not be moved or persuaded to respond to the patient's verbal productions in any way other than interpretation of their meaning.

What happens *under these circumstances* is truly remarkable. Typically, after an initial, apparently relatively uninhibited period of expression, the patient's symptoms may suddenly disappear, gradually subside in severity, or increasingly cease to concern or preoccupy him. Concomitantly, he finds free association increasingly difficult. Regularly, it is ever more persistent thoughts and intense feelings about the psychoanalyst to which he is reluctant to give verbal expression, despite the injunction to free association.

The disappearance or mitigation of the patient's symptoms, as well as the relative disappearance from his verbal productions of concern with past or current relationships outside the psychoanalysis, and the obstruction of free association are all related to his increasing preoccupation with his (usually to him unacceptable) conceptions of the psychoanalyst and the psychoanalyst's attitudes toward, feelings about, or intentions in relation to, himself; with his own (again usually to him unacceptable) attitudes toward, feelings about, or intentions in relation to, the psychoanalyst as so conceived; and with his own efforts to verify his conceptions of the psychoanalyst and to realize his aims or bring about some state of affairs in relation to the psychoanalyst.

It may be, moreover, that, given the conditions de-

scribed above, these preoccupations of the patient will
hold sway over him only or mainly for the period of the
psychoanalytic hour. Astonishingly enough, after an
hour of hesitation, strain, hints of passion, or explicit
torment, muteness, imprecations, or beseechings, the
patient may rise calmly from his incumbent position,
perhaps indicate, however fleetingly, his recognition of
the psychoanalyst as psychoanalyst, and go about his
business, relatively untroubled, only to immerse himself
once again in his *creation* the next hour. For the impression is irresistible that the patient creates something,
something circumscribed in space and time, something
out of the materials of the psychoanalysis. He makes,
according to a process of creation—that is, by using
methods—determined or made possible by the con-
straints of the psychoanalysis, something with form,
however strange, the shape of which at first is dim,
vague, as if seen always from afar through a mist, there,
lost, recovered, and lost again through many hours, but
in time looming closer, increasingly precise in outline
and rich in detail and design.

Freud did not ignore this phenomenon, damn it as a
nuisance, or exploit it to noninterpretive ends. His astonishing feat, of course, was instead to discover that
this impediment to the psychoanalysis, this obstacle to
the patient's participation in the psychoanalytic situation as defined, was, in fact, a representation of the
patient's conception of his inner world, of psychic reality, of the conflicts between imagined entities (of which
his symptoms were still another representation) now
quintessentially in the form of the transference neurosis.
As such, this representation called for interpretation no
less than the patient's free association verbal productions.

Freud's psychology would have remained relatively uninteresting if he had continued to consider the patient's reminiscences, his memories, from which he suffers, to be of actual events. Freud discovered, however, as we have noted, that patients suffer, for example, from phantasies of past experience—not, for example, from actual seductions. A phantasy is a symbol of inner reality in the form of time past, time present, or time future. (Kris has written of the life history as the patient's personal myth.) The transference neurosis is not a revival of earlier events or relationships, but of the patient's earlier, perduring conceptions of events and relationships. The transference neurosis is a symbol of these conceptions.

Psychoanalysis, despite its preoccupation with a genetic or developmental frame of reference, despite the historicism of many of its theoretical formulations, is not a science of history but a science of the symbolizing activity of the mind. Psychoanalysis cannot be concerned with the recovery—as a method it is not suitable for the study—of actual events.

The patient may refer to what is apparently the same event at different times in different contexts during a psychoanalysis. At these different times the presentations of the event and its elements are likely to differ from each other: details, emphases, conceptions of the event, and the attitudes and feelings aroused by or associated with such conceptions differ. The very history of the patient seems to change as he reconstructs it during different periods of the psychoanalysis. For during these various periods what the event and its elements mean, what the patient made and makes of them, changes. If a history is revived, it is the history of the patient's psychic reality.

We may or may not infer an actual event at that imaginary point where the patient's various representations of an event intersect, but that actual event as an entity is not knowable through, nor can it be investigated by, the method of psychoanalysis. The pathogens exorcised by psychoanalysis are not physiological processes nor historical situations but transformations, psychic representatives, of these: mental shades, memories, phantasies, conceptions, what Freud called ideas. Not reality but symbolic representations of reality. Not organism but symbolic representations of body and self. Not object-relations but symbolic representations of object-relations as conceived by the patient. Between stimulus and response, between event and behavior, falls the act of the mind. It is the act of the mind that is the object of study in psychoanalysis.

A rather vulgar notion of psychoanalysis pictures the patient reacting to what he out of error or ignorance regards as *signs* of danger, and the psychoanalyst—like a keen-eared, sharp-eyed Holmes—reacting to the patient's verbalizations, appearances, and acts as *signs* of the patient's immediate feelings or dispositions. The psychoanalyst's interventions are presumed to be based on his recognition of signs of the patient's state in the psychoanalysis as well as his recognition that the patient is interpreting signs ignorantly or erroneously. The psychoanalyst's interpretations, then, are supposed to rectify the patient's error and ignorance.

The superficial resemblance between sign and symbol —that each "stands for" something else—has tended to obscure the essential differences between them. A sign is part of, attached to, or evidence of the presence of, the particular entity or event it signifies. A sign indicates or announces. The interpretation of the significance of a sign usually determines that action and what action shall follow its perception. An elephant's footprint, a stop light, a dinner bell, a ring around the moon are signs. From the sign, we predict the entity or event it signifies. It is also true that from the entity or event, we may predict the sign. The relation between sign and entity or event is "If . . ., then. . . ." Such a relationship does not hold between a symbol, which begins with abstraction, and the conception it represents.

An alternate notion of psychoanalysis would have the patient *making a symbol* such as the transference neurosis to represent his conceptions of his inner reality, so that in the contemplation of such an objectification of his conceptions of inner reality he and the psychoanalyst may come to understand these conceptions. Psychoanalysis above all, then, studies and treats the patient who is *animal symbolicum*—maker, user, and misuser of symbols.

You appear to have been put off by my enthusiastic description of psychoanalysis. You have questions.

What kind of method of investigation confines itself to the study of a single individual? You wonder if I have become the idealist now.

The psychoanalysis of a single individual encompasses an empirical realm of many thousands of observable events, among which one may discern regularities, occurrences that under controlled conditions repeat themselves as predictably as experimental phenomena in any laboratory.

What kind of method is it whose observations can be checked by so few others?

Surely, you who know something of science, of the highly specialized conditions essential to the making of a single crucial observation, available under no other conditions, of the intricate and laboriously achieved skills—both conceptual and technical—required of the scientist, surely you will not regard the special circumstances in which psychoanalytic observations must be made and the skills required to bring these circumstances about and maintain them as arguing against psychoanalysis as a method of investigation.

I join you, however, in warning of the conceptual risks intrinsic in the use of psychotherapy—I include psychoanalysis—as a method of investigation.

Since treatment is the primary task of psychotherapy, the psychotherapist tends to focus upon what is relatively mutable and to ignore or to consign to residual categories that which is relatively immutable.

Since attention is riveted upon the symbolization function, a bias exists in the direction of attributing meaning, intention, purpose, and aim, at the expense of recognition of the impact of nonsubjective, nonsymbolic elements.

As we have seen, symbolization has both an abstractive, formulative, or conceptual aspect, on the one hand, and a suasive or communicative aspect, on the other. A psychotherapist may err in preferring to understand a patient's symbolizations almost exclusively in interpersonal terms, that is, as messages; in this case, he may miss the extent to which the patient is representing in symbolic form his own conceptions of reality—is representing, that is, his inner reality in order to give it form, to hold on to it, to contemplate it. Or a psychotherapist may err in preferring to understand a patient's symbolizations almost solely as a representation of the patient's reality without regard to suasive intent in relation to the psychotherapist. The latter inclination is likely to be associated with a tendency to reify the patient's history, as if there were one true history gradually being revealed to the psychotherapist. In fact, as I have just mentioned in discussing the transference neurosis, depending upon the patient's own state and relation to the psychotherapist at a particular time, the patient will create many histories, or, if you prefer, recreate his history many times, during psychotherapy. As he changes in psychotherapy and as his relation to the psychotherapist changes, so will his conception of his own history change. (Incidentally, do you think that such a change perhaps should be of more interest to us as psychotherapists than our current preoccupation with changes in what we call the patient's social adjustment?) Freud, referring to the intensification of sexual feelings in adolescence, suggested early in his work that previous life events are reinterpreted and invested with meaning in the light of later feelings and interests: does, then, retrospectively, such an earlier event take on the status of external trauma or pathogen in the patient's mind and in our own minds? As investigators, we should be wary of coming to simple conclusions from our psychotherapeutic work that the history of a schizophrenic person was "really" such-and-such, or that no doubt this event or that relationship as we hear about it now actually occurred in that way, then, and initiated the illness.

Let us see what Freud's model of mental illness looks like in the light of our view—also, as I have suggested, ultimately his view—of man as *animal symbolicum*.

The etiologic or pathogenic event in all psychological illness is, according to Freud, "damming up of libido," by whatever process. I see that we are in difficulty, because now you will find terms such as libido alien, difficult to understand, and even more difficult to accept. Let me try to translate this phrase "damming up of libido" in terms of the frame of reference we have been developing together.

We know that the *animal symbolicum* strives to bring about, as we say, "in reality," imagined or symbolized end-states of affairs. Such end-states are certain kinds of relations with objects—that is, other entities—conceived to be gratifying in and of themselves. Such ends are not valued as means to any other end and there is no incentive to change such an object-relationship or state of affairs should it be attained.

We may conceive that a quantity—a degree of value—is attached to this kind of end-state, which is part of its significance to its creator. An index of the value attached to an end is the extent to which a particular personality system gives priority to its attainment over the attainment of other ends. Another related quantity is the energy or effort that is allocated by the personality system or expended by the behavioral organism to overcome obstacles to realizing a valued end. Perhaps the degree of value attached to any one of a class of end-states that we characterize as sexual or as involving sexual gratification, and the energy expended or allocated to overcome obstacles to realizing such valued ends, are aspects of what Freud meant by the concept "libido."

You will no doubt want to challenge these partial translations. Are such ideas really what Freud had in mind? Barring a prolonged justification with arguments from many passages in Freud's work, with inferences concerning not only the conceptual systems from which his ideas sprung but the never-realized conceptual system to whose creation his ideas contributed—a justification which is beyond the scope of this presentation, if not my present powers as well—I can only reply to your question that I do not know, but I do not think we shall be led too far astray in adopting such translations tentatively.

"Damming up of libido," then, implies that a tendency to actualize one of a certain class of imagined or symbolized ends has met an obstacle, has been, as we say, frustrated. This tendency persists in the personality system, despite the obstacles to its fulfillment. The intensity of the tendency is represented by the value attached to the end in the sense just given, or the energy or effort the personality system continues to mobilize and direct to its realization.

Suppose you have a notion that such and such a state of affairs would be delightful. Never mind for the moment how you came to have such a notion, the nature of its origins, or to what peculiar symbolization process it owes its formation. To bring the desired state of affairs into being, you require the participation of something, usually someone, in your situation. However, while you may feel that a particular person is just right for what you have in mind, you cannot be too finicky here, since people in reality are usually not as cooperative as we would like them to be. They get lost, go away, die, are ruled out by others as inappropriate or out of bounds, or are otherwise unreliable or unavailable. Given the disagreeable, somewhat intractable nature of objective external reality, you must possess capacities enabling you to mold and alter it to suit your conception, to override, or evade, its opposition to your efforts. If one object of your desire, whatever it may be, fails you, in whatever way, you must be prepared eventually at least to find and be content with another. This is perhaps something of what Freud meant by substitution. Failing all this, finally, the environment having been completely intolerant of your notion, you must be capable of shifting a bit in your insistence that the desired end-state of affairs should be just so and of modifying your conception—not too much but just enough—so that it becomes acceptable and realizable. This maneuver is perhaps something of what Freud meant by sublimation.

To some extent, whether an object is "there," is available, depends on your particular conception and symbolic representation of it. Through your own symbolic activity, you create (or are unable to create) the object you desire. To some extent, it is your commitment to a particular symbolic representation of the desired object that may make substitution of another for it difficult or impossible; it is your commitment to a particular symbolic representation of a desirable end-state that may make modification of it difficult or impossible. So, even where the obstacle seems to exist in the situation, it may be constituted to a large extent in fact by symbolic processes.

Now, as if matters were not complicated enough, as *animal symbolicum* you have not confined yourself to one such notion of the desirable. You appear to delight in generating, or actually to be compelled to generate, many such notions. Some of these symbolizations compete in the personality system with others for allocation of energy or effort. Some of these symbolizations conflict with or rule out others; that is, the end-state of affairs represented by one is or seems incompatible with that represented by another.

The success of your efforts, as we have seen, depends upon the cooperation of external reality; that failing, you may manage to the limits of your talents in this direction with the expedients of substitution and sub-

limation. However, now we see that the success of your
efforts also depends upon the cooperation and organization of a variety of kinds of symbolization systems constituting your personality. Failure of the requisite degree of organization of various tendencies, of subordination of one tendency to another, may also constitute an
obstacle to your efforts. The refusal to give consent, the
prohibition we associate with such a system of symbolizations as we conceive the superego to be may also constitute an obstacle to your efforts. Associated with your
notion of delight and in opposition to it you may anticipate or experience a state of affairs in which the value
attached not to some external object-representation but
to your own self-representation is diminished. We call
this a threat to self-esteem or narcissism, that is, a threat
to some desired relation to your own self as object: as
animal symbolicum, you are capable of conceiving relations to yourself or to your self-representation. Here,
clearly, the obstacle is an internalized symbolic process
or symbolic representation.

Let us sum up the kinds of obstacles that may frus-
trate you in seeking the attainment of your ends. One,
the external world is not compliant, or your symbolizations of it create it not so. Two, you are, to whatever
extent, incapable of substitution and sublimation.
Three, as a behavioral organism, through enfeeblement
or by innate endowment, you lack energic, cognitive, or
other resources or equipment that you require to overcome obstacles, to master your situation and so to adapt
to it. (Freud, in this connection, referred to enfeeblement of the ego due to organic illness or to constitu-
tional factors.) Four, your personality system is in-
adequately organized to mediate among tendencies competing for allocation of effort to their fulfillment, or it

includes symbolizations incompatible with, and oppos-
ing the allocation of effort to the fulfillment of, a particular tendency.

I wish for your sake that we were finished with this
dismal catalogue. After all, if the world is so disagreeable that even your considerable talent for substitution
and sublimation is inordinately taxed, or if your talent
in these directions is somewhat less than you would like
so that you find it difficult to manage the complications
created by even a moderately difficult world, then you
are in trouble. You can tolerate the frustration of your
strivings, but only up to a certain limit. You will struggle, maneuver, fiddle, and fuss, but beyond a certain
point you want what you want. As an *animal symbolicum,* you are immensely impressed by your conceptions
of the way things ought to be and exhibit an astonishing
fidelity and devotion in remaining attached to these
conceptions. Nevertheless, on top of difficulties from
without, you must also suffer opposition from within.
And, as if that weren't enough, your situation is im-
measurably complicated by the vicissitudes of development.

Development forces upon you the necessity to exchange one conception of the desirable for another. If
you refuse, if you are not ready for, such renunciation,
we may term this after Freud an inhibition of development. If you agree to make such a renunciation, but
rather unwillingly, remaining attached to the abrogated
notion and returning to it whenever the obduracy of
external reality or your own limitations lead to your
frustration in connection with later notions, we may
speak with Freud of fixation and regression. Such inhibition of development, fixation, regression, create and
exacerbate disharmony in your relations with others or

within yourself or both, in any event, increasing the likelihood of frustration. If at a certain time of life a concatenation of circumstances rather abruptly contrives to increase the clamor of a particular tendency to be realized, increases the significance of an internalized symbolic representation, disturbing your previous degree of devotion to this tendency or symbolic representation and the careful arrangements made for its relations to other tendencies or symbolic representations, and straining both the patience of external reality and your own capacities for substitution and sublimation, then we may remember Freud's references to the frustration following upsurges of libido at adolescence or menopause. Even if you are enthusiastic about exchanging one kind of satisfaction for another, renouncing one goal in favor of the adoption of a new one, you may find that the new ideal is incompatible or conflicts with other of your rather entrenched ideals. (Freud writes of people "falling ill . . . as often when they discard an ideal as when they seek to attain it.") Since you must change—the world in which you live expects it; in becoming yourself, you internalize these expectations as your own; the behavioral organism matures—since change you must, with all the risk such change entails, then you are lucky indeed if you do not fall ill in the course of your lifetime.

Mental illness or illness from the point of view of the personality system is the morbid process—and the effects of attempts to recover from it—initiated by some degree and duration of frustration of a wish to attain a symbolized desirable state of affairs that remains unmitigated by adaptive mastery of external reality, substitution, or sublimation. (The desirable state of affairs symbolized may, of course, come to involve a conception of avoidance of, or escape from, harm or threat.) The obstacle to the attainment of a desirable state of affairs itself is with respect to a mental illness most significantly—from the point of view we have developed here—constituted by or originated in aspects of symbolic processes. The response to frustration constitutes the morbid process. The process is morbid because, with respect to attaining gratifying states of affairs in reality, it is destined to fail. Differences in the response to frustration, as well as in the attempts to recover from the morbid process, differentiate psychological illnesses from each other.

One response—characteristic of what we call neurosis—is to give up your efforts to attain a gratifying state of affairs in reality, but to rest content with imagining such a state of affairs, that is, with phantasy. To use Freud's language, you may withdraw cathexis or libido from current reality object-representations, and invest such cathexis or libido in the object-representations of phantasy. In other words, for you the object-representations of external reality appear to have less and less significance with respect to *particular kinds* of aims or goal-strivings. (Keep in mind that this describes a circumscribed process and not the entire personality.) At the same time instead you attribute greater and greater significance to the object-representations of inner reality. Having little incentive to cling to progressive conceptions of the desirable that have met such an unhappy fate, you relinquish these. The symbolizations of phantasy tend to find their best material in other regressive conceptions of the desirable, remnants of past eras of your life—"better days." These conceptions are revalued and effort is allocated to the creation of phantasies of their fulfillment.

However, there is not much gratification in phantasy. What there is is illusory, and even an *animal symbolicum* finds it difficult to rest content with that. The regressive conceptions of the desirable, perhaps in part as a result of their characteristics as symbolizations, in turn begin to be associated with impulsions to actualization in reality. Such a development may be viewed as a kind of attempt to recover from the turning-away from object-representations of external reality initiated by the pathogenic frustration. However, the regressive conceptions conflict with other conceptions of the desirable in the personality system. Symbolic maneuvers—the so-called defenses—aim at the extrusion of these disturbing regressive conceptions. It is important to realize that, as such writers as Isaacs and Schafer have pointed out, defenses are not "mechanisms"—a word borrowed from positivistic terminology—but are themselves symbolic processes. In fact, defenses are phantasies, representing conceptions of internal events, of contents or objects imagined within or without; representing conceptions of imagined interactions with, imagined location of, and imagined operations upon, self-representations and object-representations. Differences in these maneuvers or defenses differentiate to a large extent between the various neuroses and account (along with manifestations of the regressive conceptions) for the form of neurotic symptoms. Neurotic symptoms are understandable, then, as attempts at recovery, as efforts—which are only partially successful and which often lead to considerable pain—to struggle against the largely silent, morbid neurotic process.

The response to frustration characteristic of psychosis is to withdraw cathexis or libido from current reality object-representations and from object-representations in phantasy as well. As Freud is careful to point out in his discussion of the Schreber case, this does not mean that a person insofar as he is psychotic has *no* interest in reality or phantasy. Withdrawal from reality has a more specific meaning than is usually attributed to it. It means only that with respect to particular kinds of aims or goal-strivings—Freud classifies these as sexual—a person insofar as he is psychotic attributes less and less significance to current reality object-representations or to object-representations in phantasy, and greater and greater significance to his own self-representation or to an undifferentiated state (perhaps devoid of symbolization processes?) in which neither object-representations nor self-representation exist or in which, to the extent such representations have some form (no matter how rudimentary), neither has such significance.

Megalomania, with its narcissistic overvaluation of the self, is one manifestation of this abandonment of other objects in favor of the self. Preoccupation with end of the world catastrophe may represent the patient's experience of the loss of all other objects in current external reality or in inner reality.

According to Freud's conception of schizophrenia, the schizophrenic person's use of language, hallucinations, and delusions are all evidence of processes of reconstruction or attempts at recovery, however dysfunctional their consequences. In an effort to return to the world of objects, the patient attributes to words the significance of the objects to which words are ordinarily attached. As unconscious thing-representations—sensory images—are subjected to primary processes of condensation and displacement, so word-representations rather than thing-representations come to be subjected to such processes. Words are treated by the patient as things.

Delusions and hallucinations represent in part efforts to create a new reality, in the form of thought or image, to replace the rejected reality. The new reality has elements at least more favorable to gratification than the rejected reality. In hallucination, object-representations once again are significant especially with respect to wish-fulfilling phantasies; but they pass into consciousness as images without benefit of secondary thought processes, which have been disrupted by the morbid psychotic process.

Although there is much to say and to question about this model of mental illness, many of you no doubt feeling that as a model of neurosis it is limited perhaps to hysteria and that especially as a conception of schizophrenia it is neither the most important nor most useful model available to us, I see that our time is up. In order to prepare us for an account of another conception of schizophrenia, it would, I believe, be especially useful to consider Freud's ideas about language, consciousness, and unconsciousness. In these ideas there seems to me to be still another meaning of cathexis, different from any we have mentioned, and leading to another idea of mental illness. As you have perhaps already guessed, I am in fact primarily interested in discussing these two conceptions of schizophrenia because such a discussion provides us with the occasion to consider symbolic functioning and consciousness. Perhaps, then, at our next meeting, we shall devote ourselves to this subject.

3: Symbolic Process and Consciousness

Ladies and gentlemen:

I find my thoughts again turning to language. What are your views about language? Perhaps you have no views; you take language for granted. So do many of us in psychiatry despite the fact that we use words in the treatment of illness. Perhaps you think of words as useful and ornamental tags affixed to sensory images. Words, then, are labels upon a prior, independently formed, sensory experience. The meaning of a word lies ultimately in the image or images or relation between images to which it refers.

I think it must have been from a notion about language something like this that Sullivan was led in his 1939 paper, "The Language of Schizophrenia," to question in a fantastical paragraph the idea that language and thought are intimately related. "I have for years," he wrote, "contemplated the experiment of having a child taught one language for speech and another for writing. This would be quite feasible, although some persistent attitudes make us inept teachers. Such an individual would probably think as well as, if not better than, most of us do. He would not be misled about the intimate relation of language to thought. The fact that one or the other of his languages happened to decorate as grace notes what was going on in his mind would be to him clearly irrelevant."

Others, such as Cassirer, Whorf, and Sapir, have disagreed, writing persuasively that language is not merely laid down upon experience, but is rather constitutive of experience. Stated briefly: language, to some extent at

73

least, determines how and what we experience. Similarly, Lidz, in his work on schizophrenia, has held that the language we learn determines how we think.

Freud, as is true with so many lines of his thought, seems to have begun with the older, apparently simpler, naive realism. Without ever explicitly abandoning it, he nevertheless gradually permitted what was already also in him to emerge: a complex, and, what seems to me I must admit, a more sophisticated, truer view, prefiguring developments in science he was not himself to know.

In his early monograph on impairments of speech, *On Aphasia,* as part of an effort to account for various types of aphasia, Freud differentiated thing-representations or thing concepts from word-representations or word concepts. A thing-representation he defined as a complex of sensory qualities with various origins—visual, acoustic, kinaesthetic, tactile, and so on. A word-representation he defined as a complex of images of the word as spoken, written, read, heard, and so on. The connection between thing-representation and word-representation occurs, Freud supposed, through a linkage of the sound element of the word-representation and the visual element of the thing-representation.

Freud then distinguished in terms of function rather than localized anatomic lesion among verbal aphasias, asymbolic aphasias, and agnostic aphasias. In verbal aphasia, the symptoms are various kinds of motor or expressive difficulties with language. Freud held that some functional relation between the separate elements of the word-representation—for example, between the images of the word as heard and the word as spoken— was disturbed in verbal aphasia. In asymbolic aphasia, the symptoms are various kinds of failure to receive or understand speech (understand in the sense of relating a word to the thing to which the word refers). Freud held that some functional relation between word-representation and thing-representation—for example, between the image of the spoken word and the visual image of the thing—was disturbed in asymbolic aphasia. In agnostic aphasia, there is a disturbance in the relation between the elements of the thing-representation—for example, between a tactile image and a visual image of the thing—such that things are not recognized, and incitement to spontaneous speech arising from associations between the elements of the thing-representation does not occur.

I do not mean to distract us from our central concern in these lectures by a discussion of aphasia, which is still a mystery in medicine, largely, perhaps, because we do not understand language. However, important tendencies in Freud's thought in this monograph were fateful for his later work; they are relevant to our understanding of a mental illness such as schizophrenia, and perhaps other mental illnesses as well.

Freud was dissatisfied with the notion that the type of aphasia depends upon the localization of discrete lesions. He conceived rather of a speech apparatus whose parts are interdependently related. This apparatus functions at different levels of organization. A higher level of organization or functioning requires more capacity than a lower one. Impairments of speech depend upon characteristics of the entire speech apparatus—for example, its general level of functioning as that is affected by any event depriving the speech apparatus of capacity and therefore acting to depress its level of functioning. In this conception, Freud was probably influenced by the neurologist Hughlings Jackson, who stressed the importance of the principle of hierarchy of organization or level of function for understanding bio-logical phenomena.

Freud, therefore, may be said to have thought as a system analyst or system theorist, long before this was fashionable, and to have conceived of impairment or disease as depending not upon localized lesions in, or the state of some part of, a system but rather upon the general level of function, or the state, of the entire sys-tem. In moving from a consideration of the neuro-physiological system to a consideration of the person-ality system, he retained these habits of thought, and some of his great theoretical contributions are related to them.

Twenty-four years later, in his essay, "The Uncon-scious," Freud, now concerned with the so-called psychic apparatus, conceived of conscious and uncon-scious as two separate systems, each with its own dis-tinct characteristics. Secondary process thinking, for example, was characteristic of the conscious system and primary process thinking of the unconscious system. (As you no doubt remember, he later abandoned this formu-lation for that of the structural theory—the id, ego, and superego becoming subsystems of functions within the personality system with conscious and unconscious pro-cesses possible in any one of the subsystems.) However, in this same essay, Freud debated whether it might be more useful to conceptualize the difference between consciousness and unconsciousness in terms of a func-tional change of state of the psychic apparatus—as we might say, of the system of symbolic processes and internalized symbolic forms.

Though apparently rejecting this last alternative, Freud later in the same essay distinguished between a conscious representation and an unconscious one in terms of the presence or absence of language as symbolic activity and the higher level of organization such activity makes possible. He supposed that a conscious representation comprises both thing-representation and the word-representation belonging to it, while an unconscious representation is a thing-representation alone. In the system unconscious, Freud thought, there was no language, but only the representations of things to which language refers. For thoughts or wishes to become conscious, thing-representations must be, in Freud's terms, hypercathected by becoming linked to word-representations. That is, thing-representations come to have greater value or significance with respect to the goals of the personality system and come to be associated with increased effort mobilized for the attainment of such goals through linkage with word-representations. According to Freud, then, the possibility of a "higher psychical organization," consciousness, in which primary process can be succeeded by secondary process, depends upon a so-called hypercathexis of thing-representations, which requires the introduction of meaningful symbolic activity.

A conception of the psychic apparatus or personality system as moving back and forth between different functional states or levels of organization is implied in these formulations. I became especially interested in this conception while working with some schizophrenic patients. I was struck with the rapidity with which states of consciousness appeared to alter in these patients. Transitions from lucidity to confusion and back to lucidity again, from coherent rational communication to bizarre representation of thoughts in actions rather than words, from states of quiet to states of frenzied excitement, occurred often in the middle of a sentence or from minute to minute in a psychotherapy session. I found that I and the patient were soon in difficulty when I could not keep up—if I failed to recognize such rapid alterations in levels of functioning when talking with a schizophrenic person. This is fatiguing work, about the most fatiguing I have ever done. (Pious has given an especially sensitive account of this process. I recommend to you his paper, "A Hypothesis About the Nature of Schizophrenic Behavior," which you might like to study after the case histories of Freud as a model of clinical research or of the integration of theory and clinical observation.)

In order to realize what "levels of organization or functioning" means, think for a minute about the various degrees of wakefulness we all experience. Perhaps we rarely know the state of being fully awake to which Thoreau referred when he wrote: "Morning is when I am awake and there is a dawn in me. Moral reform is the effort to throw off sleep. Why is it that men give so poor an account of their day if they have not been slumbering? They are not such poor calculators. If they had not been overcome with drowsiness, they would have performed something. The millions are awake enough for physical labor; but only one in a million is awake enough for effective intellectual exertion, only one in a hundred millions to a poetic or divine life. To be awake is to be alive. I have never yet met a man who was quite awake. How could I have looked him in the face?" There is no doubt that Thoreau meant that being fully awake requires an exertion of effort to move from one level of functioning to another.

Compare with being fully awake your state of mind while listening to this lecture—occasional reveries and blanking out alternating with focused attention. Think of drowsiness—the strange, fleeting, compelling images that are so difficult to recapture upon reawakening. Think of falling asleep—the gradual fading into shadow of surrounding things, even as a heavy sense of your own body remains. Then part of your body too disappears, while other parts remain in ghostly isolation; your body becomes almost gone, an ache here or throbbing there reminding you of it—but does it seem quite your body?—before you fall asleep. Think of some dreams—the vivid, hallucinatory scenes, the intense feelings, as though you were many times more alive than in this muted world of sober thought. Think of other dreams—the terrifying nightmare in which you struggle trapped, from which you feel you will never awaken. Think of deep dreamless sleep.

Federn and Pious have discussed similarly altered states of consciousness reported by the schizophrenic patient. He looks upon a world without color, a world he recognizes but from which he feels estranged. It has lost familiarity; it does not feel real to him. He looks detachedly at his arm; he can test reality, he knows it is his arm, he touches it, he traces its connection to the shoulder, but in the state we call depersonalization it does not feel like his arm. The same patient, perhaps confused and disorganized, does not use words but rather images, feelings, and actions to represent meanings as you or I use such materials to represent meanings in a dream. Hallucinating, frightened, fascinated, he may feel trapped in a world of vivid images from which he cannot escape. Think of that same patient lurching and staggering from one word to another, and suddenly blank, motionless, from words to silence. Think of the strained attention and effort such a patient may then bring to the creation of some order, any kind of order—

how he focuses on words, how he weaves and strings them, how he scrutinizes each word, how he doubts and backs up and repeats, refusing to let anything pass without clearing and placing and clarifying and connecting it. Is that not how you or I might try to awaken ourselves from a nightmare?

This formulation—levels of organization or functioning—may be applied to the personality system. In a personality system with well differentiated subsystems (for example, id, ego, superego, and ego-ideal), various functions or types of symbolizations with different characteristics and aims are organized and regulated differently. Each type of symbolization is invoked when relevant, inhibited to the extent irrelevant, or, in other words, enjoys different priorities in different circumstances. Such subsystems, each well organized and well differentiated, may conflict—as in the neuroses.

It is sometimes, although not invariably, difficult to classify the symbolizations of the schizophrenic person in this way. Rather than conflict between well organized, well differentiated subsystems, sometimes different types of symbolizations appear to melt together in an undifferentiated symbolization matrix. For example, a neurotic patient's symbolizations may translate roughly as follows: "I want to cross the street, but I do not think I should; I have a feeling it would be wrong to do so, although as a matter of fact I recognize that in reality there is no danger in doing so and that, if I am in fact going to get what I want, I must cross the street." At times, the schizophrenic patient sounds like that; at other times, these meanings have all been strangely simplified or homogenized. The schizophrenic patient's symbolizations translate roughly as follows: "I should not cross the street." But the various meanings—"I should not cross the street because there is danger I might be run over; I should not cross the street because I feel that doing so would be wrong; I do not want to cross the street because I am enjoying myself where I am"—are not separated. The schizophrenic patient may seem to mean all these things at once, or perhaps seems not to recognize clearly that these are different possibilities in what he symbolizes. Similarly, the schizophrenic patient may represent in one way or another the absence of something, without clearly distinguishing between: "I do not like it" and "In reality it is not there."

I am reminded by this discussion of a type of experience I have had working with a schizophrenic patient in psychotherapy. I might have responded to his proposition "I should not cross the street" by imagining a harsh, forbidding superego inhibiting cognitive or expressive aims. I might then have communicated in some way to my patient—perhaps by asking, in response to his proposition, "and what is that all about?"—that I thought he might be overly severe with himself. He might have for some reason accepted my formulation. Both of us would then suffer an unpleasant surprise. In attempting to abandon this apparently overmoral position, my patient would act as if he now could not tell the difference between a street that was safe to cross and one that was not and would become entirely unclear about whether or not he wanted to cross any particular street. In other words, the symbolization "I should not cross the street" had been, unknown to either of us, performing a variety of undifferentiated functions, and in urging him to abrogate it I had indeed made possible for baby to be thrown out with bathwater. What sounds moral to us, in other words, may be serving cognitive and expressive functions also. Having this somewhat gross means of steering oneself is better than having no means at all, as my patient—more than a little angry about the mess in which I had landed him—soon made clear to me by treating me with my interpretations as a dangerous enemy.

We might say that cognitive, moral, and expressive symbolizations remain for such a personality system at such times part of an undifferentiated symbolization matrix, or in other terms that ego, superego, and id are, at least some of the time, relatively undifferentiated. Such a personality system may function intermittently or relatively continuously at a lower level of organization—characterized by simplification, homogeneity, or lack of differentiation—than that characteristic of the personality system with well differentiated subsystems. As William Pious has suggested to me recently, and as I think Federn implied by his concept "ego states," a number of functional states or levels of organization of the personality system, from fully differentiated to completely undifferentiated, are in this view possible not only from person to person but within the same person.

If the highest levels of organization are characterized by the secondary process, and intermediate levels of organization by the primary process, may we not conceive that the lowest levels of organization are characterized by asymbolia, that state dreaded above all others by the *animal symbolicum*? It is something like this asymbolic level perhaps to which Pious refers in his concept of the nadir suffered by the schizophrenic person—that lowest moment of emptiness and blankness for which the patient has no words and, perhaps, indeed, no form of symbolization at all.

If higher levels of functioning are characterized by

consciousness, should we conclude that the degree of consciousness, as implied by Freud, is related to the value or significance that object-representations have with respect to the goal-strivings of the personality system and the amount of effort mobilized to actualize such goal-strivings? But, then, does it not also make sense to think of the degree of consciousness as related to the availability of energy, effort, or capacity required to move from a lower level of organization to a higher one—just as energy is required to move from one orbit to another in the atomic realm? This way of thinking is characteristic of Federn and Pious; they have followed up the implications in Freud's formulations concerning the functional state of a system in their conceptions of schizophrenia.

It is clear, then, that such words as libido and cathexis may be used, on the one hand, to mean value or significance with respect to goal-striving, or energy allocated to the actualization of a conception of the desirable; on the other hand, such words may be used—as by Federn —to mean capacity to move from one functional state or level of organization to another. In the first usage, we are concerned with the actualization of a conception of the desirable; in the second usage, we are concerned with the achievement of a form or level of symbolization. It is unfortunate that the same words have been used to represent such different ideas, and it is important to be clear what meaning is intended on any particular occasion of the use of these words.

According to a conception of schizophrenia exemplified in the works of Federn and Pious, the etiologic or pathogenic event is not frustration, as in the model of mental illness we discussed at our last meeting, but impoverishment. In the libido-cathexis terminology, libido (in its first meaning) is not "dammed up" in the personality system but (in its second meaning) is lost from the personality system. In other words, the problem is not a relative excess of value, significance, or effort, which, meeting obstacles to actualizing a desirable relation to the object in reality, is therefore redirected to the self. The problem is rather a deficiency of some capacity required for the organization and functioning of the personality system. The pathogenic event is not an interference with actualization of a conception of a desirable end state of affairs. The pathogenic event is rather the depletion of the capacity of the personality system to achieve, to sustain, or, having lost it, to regain a higher level of organization or functioning.

What is the nature of this capacity? It is difficult to formulate it clearly. I shall risk losing your attention while I make a first, stumbling attempt to solve this problem—necessarily leading us into a thicket of unclear sentences which adequately represent my still half-formed thoughts. For what is needed here is just what we do not yet have—an adequate conceptualization of symbolic process. Anyway, those of you who remain with me can join me in claiming that at least we have made a beginning in this difficult area.

My first thoughts are based on the differentiation, stressed by Hartmann, between the "cathexis of an object-directed ego function and the cathexis of an object representation" and between the cathexis of the self-representation and the cathexis of ego functions. In other words, we may distinguish between the attribution of value or significance (with respect to the attainment of desirable end-states of affairs), first, to an object-representation; second, to the self-representation; third, to an ego function or, indeed, to any of the various kinds of functions of the personality system—specifically, to any aspect or any kind of the symbolization processes constituting the personality system. Such symbolization processes may also involve either object-representations or self-representation. That is, conceptions of either the object world or of the self may be represented by symbolic forms.

Therefore, effort may be allocated, first, to the attainment of a desirable relation to the object world; second, to the attainment of a desirable relation to the self; third, to the achievement at higher levels of organization of symbolic representations of the object world or of the self. Since the resources of the personality system (as of any system) are never unlimited at any moment of time, these different requirements for the allocation of effort may compete with each other.

On the basis of some such formulation as this, probably, Federn came to the conclusion that, when ego functioning was impaired, the expenditure of libido in object-relations resulted in an exacerbation of such impairment and that limitation of such expenditure was necessary to bring about an improvement in ego functioning. However, I do not find the relation between object-relations and ego functioning so simple. I cannot accept either that one is always enhanced at the expense of the other or that, on the contrary, and this may surprise some of you, that improvement of object-relations always results in a higher level of ego functioning or that a higher level of ego functioning is always followed by an improvement in object-relations.

Our conceptualizations appear, then, to be insufficient to the problems we are investigating. However, let us tentatively say that capacity to achieve, maintain or, having lost, to regain higher levels of organization or functioning of the personality system is essentially the availability and allocation of effort to achieve, maintain or, having lost, to regain higher levels of symbolization activity. We may distinguish this capacity from that which depends upon the availability and allocation of effort to bring about desirable end-states of affairs "in reality."

You are quick, and rightly so, to object that I have merely substituted one rather vague phrase for another, and in response to your prodding I shall make an effort to be somewhat more specific about the idea "levels of symbolization activity." Not without some trepidation about the distance we are moving from our starting point, and the ever-widening scope of our inquiry.

Subsystems of personality are classes of processes in time, not structures in space (as Parsons and Loewald among others have emphasized). Each subsystem is defined by the end toward which the processes constituting it are oriented, by the requirement of the personality system these processes are organized to meet, and not by particular "equipment"—so-called apparatuses of perception, memory, etc., which may provide elements or serve as resources for any subsystem. I agree here with Schur who has justified conceiving the id to be a subsystem of the personality, with its own characteristic organization of elements such as perception and memory (which have been for others the distinguishing characteristics exclusively of the ego as a subsystem). The wish, for example, depends upon the existence of a cathected memory, a representation of a past experience, which seeks recreation in the present.

Meditating upon ideas suggested to me by Loewald's wise and beautiful paper, "Superego and Time," I come upon the following formulations.

The function of the ego is to create the psychic present in anticipation of the psychic future. The ego is a
system of cognitive symbolizations, means of mastery,
adaptation, understanding, and control, to be used in
the attainment of a range of unspecified ends in the
future. The generation of such cognitive symbolizations
proceeds according to the secondary process, and action
in the psychic reality created by them is regulated by
the reality principle.

The function of the id is to evoke the psychic past in
order to recreate it in the psychic present. The id is a
system of symbolizations of internal states, taking the
form of memories of gratification or deprivation, which
call upon the personality system to recreate or destroy
them in the form of the psychic present. The generation
of such symbolizations proceeds according to the primary process, and action in the psychic reality created
by them is regulated by the pleasure and unpleasure
principles.

The function of the superego is to create the psychic
future out of the manifold possibilities immanent in the
psychic present. The superego is a system of moral evaluations, of representations of the consequences of
choosing one alternative rather than another. I do not
know how to describe the process according to which
such symbolizations are generated: the act of judgment
in consent or prohibition; the appreciation of the negative; the sense of free will, that there are choices to be
made and that it is both necessary and possible to make
them; the imaginative anticipation of consequences to
relationships with another or others—all are part of this
process, which I suspect develops as a dialogue with
internalized others and continues eventually as a dialogue with oneself. Action in the psychic reality created

by such symbolizations is regulated by moral standards or criteria, which give priority in considering alternatives to the consequences for a system of which one feels and chooses to be a part, and by internal sanctions such as guilt, but also by the sense of being loved from within (about which Schafer has written in his paper on the loving superego).

The function of the ego-ideal is to evoke the psychic past in order to recreate it in the psychic future. The ego-ideal is a system of recollections of the numinous, the awesome, the sacred, often in the form of ultimate values and nonempirical beliefs, which call upon the personality system to actualize them in the form of the psychic future. The generation of such ideals proceeds according to the primary process, according to mythic thought, and action in the psychic reality created by such symbolizations is regulated by internal sanctions such as pride and shame.

Have we then arrived at another formulation of the relation between consciousness and symbolic functioning? I am led by my experiences with schizophrenic patients, some of which I have reported to you, to consider that the differentiation of subsystems of the personality—the consequent shifts in commitment from one kind of symbolic process to another, the tension that comes with the recognition of difference and the requirement to choose among types of symbolic process, the clash of one symbolic process against another as these compete for priority and resources—whatever the problems it brings, is a step from a lower level of organization to a higher level of organization. That step is necessary for movement from a lower to a higher level of consciousness. From recreation to creation—from the recreation of the past in the present or future, to the creation of the present for the sake of the future, and to the creation of the future out of the possibilities of the present—is a step from a lower to a higher level of consciousness.

Because each of these subsystems may fluctuate in the level of consciousness of its functioning even from moment to moment, much more over longer periods of time, we must visualize the possibility of different ego, id, superego, ego-ideal processes even in the same individual. Of course, then, we should not speak of "his id," "his ego," etc., reifying a fluctuant process—which moves not only in time but up and down levels of consciousness—as though it were a structure in space and constant in character as well.

Because man lives in a symbolic world, a psychic reality, he may recreate his past, and even more may create his present and his future; to that extent he has forged in symbolic process a new instrumentality for guaranteeing his relative autonomy from the merely physical world and freed himself from being a mere reactive creature there.

When I say "recreate" or "create," what do I mean? I mean, first of all, the act of abstraction, the evolution of a conception of, rather than a reaction to, reality. We know from psychoanalysis that certain capacities are necessary for this act of abstraction to occur; the maturation of innate equipment is required; the development of processes that establish and control boundaries and mediate transactions across such boundaries is especially necessary. A reaction to reality must be inhibited if it is to become a response to a conception of reality, and for this a time boundary is required. Delay must be interposed between the pressure of the situation (whether body or environment) and the response to it. Further, a boundary must be established between the inner and outer, for what is outer must be taken in, there transformed to conception, and that conception ultimately perhaps represented by an objectification in a material medium. The symbolic form so created partakes of both inner and outer and unites them.

Secondly, I mean then by "recreate" or "create" the act of giving form to a conception.

A symbol is a form, which is created. I shall call the particular resources used in making a kind of symbolic form a "symbolic medium." A symbol insofar as it is a symbol represents an abstraction, which I call a conception. This "conception" is what I believe Freud meant by "idea." The relation between symbol and conception is connotation. A conception may function as a reference to a particular object or event that is an exemplar of the conception; such an exemplar may be called a referent. The relation between conception and exemplar is denotation. In other words, a symbol may represent or connote a class (the conception); a conception may be used to denote or refer to a particular member of a class.

Connotation may occur in the absence of denotation. A symbol may represent a conception in the absence of any exemplar of it. This characteristic—the evocation of the invisible—is the sine qua non of symbolic process. A symbol may represent that which is not there, which is not here, which is not now. A symbol never represents a thing but it may represent a conception of a thing. It may also represent a conception of a no-thing.

A symbol is intrinsically ambiguous; it is always potentially capable of representing more than one conception (i.e., having more than one meaning) at the same time, since there is no necessary connection between a symbol and the conception it represents. (Kris has an interesting discussion of this ambiguity in relation to aesthetics.) A symbol, therefore, always involves the audience to which it is presented in uncertainty, choice, freedom. Increasing the adequacy of prior information or experience held by the audience does not decrease the ambiguity of the symbol. In fact, "information" or "experience" may simply make clear to what an extent a symbol is ambiguous—that is, how many meanings it may or does have on a particular occasion. The need, as in scientific discourse, to make agreements to restrict the meanings a symbol will have in a particular context or type of presentation, and the difficulties in maintaining such agreements, are eloquent testimonials to the intrinsic ambiguity of symbols.

A symbol, because of its intrinsic ambiguity, is capable of achieving many aims at once; from this multi-functionality arise both its power and mischief. A symbol may evoke at the same moment a variety of conceptions. As I have commented already, "multiple determination"—a concept originating in a positivistic frame of reference—is a misnomer; as an idea, it represents, I believe, a recognition of the intrinsic ambiguity of symbols. That, in a system characterized by symbolic process, phenomena have multiple meanings is a consequence of symbolicity.

I repeat, because it is so frequently not understood, that a symbol does not stand for a particular object or event; a symbol does not denote or refer to a referent. It always represents an abstraction—for example, a class or category (ideational conception), or a configuration, pattern, or schema (imaged conception). We infer ideational conceptions. An ideational conception cannot be known directly. An ideational conception is known only through some symbolic representation of it. If we attempt to discover the conception, we simply translate from one symbolic representation of it to another, from one symbolic form to another, using one symbolic medium instead of another.

The abstraction is a free invention, constrained by the character of particular objects or events on the one hand, and the capacities of the abstracting mind on the other, but not determined solely by either. A conception is not determined by any particular exemplifications of it. The abstraction is functionally, if not actually, the result of a decision about a way to order or organize the world of things-as-they-are—what aspects of the world of things-as-they-are are significant and what significance shall be attributed to them. An abstraction orders or organizes events; it is a way of apprehending events (through imaged conceptions) or comprehending events (through ideational conceptions). That is to say, apprehended or comprehended events are exemplars of conceptions and are discriminable as such. An abstraction (always in some symbolic form representing it) may be evoked in the absence of any concrete, existential exemplar or embodiment of it.

At the level of proto-conception, what is abstracted is the value, essence, or impact of a particular moment, object, or event.

At a higher level of abstraction, what is abstracted is a class or category, of which any exemplar is a member. Membership in the class is determined by criteria which make possible the designation of any new particular as member or nonmember of the class.

Essentially, what psychoanalysts mean by "object constancy" is the formation of one such class concept: an identity class. All particulars no matter how disparate in their appearance, impact, or emotional value are conceived to be members of one class—the class constituted by an identity. (In this sense, a proper name is a symbol, although it is sometimes claimed that it is not a symbol because such a proper name is—mistakenly—conceived to refer not to an abstraction but rather to only one concrete phenomenon.)

It is not always made clear in psychoanalytic writing whether self-representation or object-representations are conceptions of self or object or particular kinds of symbols of such conceptions. In any event, the self-representation, if conception, is—as used in psychoanalytic theory—such an identity class; if symbol, it symbolizes such an identity class. I recommend, although such a recommendation goes against common usage, using the terms self-conception and object-conception for the "idea" of self or object and the terms self-representation and object-representation for the symbolic forms that represent such conceptions. Actually, we never "know" a self-concept or object-concept directly, but only in some symbolic form representing it.

A simple conception is relatively undifferentiated. The complexity of a conception is measured not by its generality or inclusiveness alone but by the number of differentiable criterial attributes, relations, or subclasses defining it. The status of a class in a hierarchy of classes —in supraordinate and subordinate relation to each other—may be, at higher levels of abstraction, identifiable. The class, then, receives its character from the nature of the hierarchy to which it belongs, from its relation to other classes, some of which are subclasses of it and some of which include it as subclass.

A parallel development occurs from the level of abstraction at which a class is a category of "things" (e.g., objects) to the level of abstraction at which a class is a category of acts (e.g., functions or performances), a category of "relations" between "things" (e.g., cathexes), or a category of logical operations upon entities (e.g., primary or secondary process).

At the highest level of abstraction, that of pure conception, a class is a category of conceptions—as in mathematical logic, a class may be a category of any entities satisfying certain criteria even if these involve no perceptual attributes whatsoever.

It may seem to you that the more complex and the more abstract the conception, the higher the level of consciousness. But I suggest that movement from a lower to a higher level of consciousness follows the creation of the form through which the conception is at the same time itself created, contemplated, and comprehended.

Symbolic forms are necessary for the formation and maintenance of complex conceptions, for the contemplation of such conceptions, and thus, through the embodiment of increasingly complex conceptions in forms it is possible to retain and to contemplate, for the achievement of higher levels of consciousness.

There are two kinds of symbolic presentations: rational forms and apparitional forms. The language of science or instrumental action, Parsons' cognitive symbolization, and Freud's secondary process exemplify the presentation of symbols in rational form. The forms of art, Parsons' expressive symbolization, and Freud's primary process exemplify the presentation of symbols in apparitional form. The term "apparitional form" is used because such forms "appear" in space-time, though the "appearance" be illusory, in the sense that a virtual image in a mirror is illusory—for example, as described by Langer, the virtual powers created in dance, the virtual time created in music, the virtual space created in plastic art, the virtual events created in poesis, the virtual history created in literature, and the virtual present created in drama.

It is especially characteristic of a presentation of symbols in rational form that the relation between symbol and conception is arbitrary; they do not resemble each other; they do not share membership in a class. It is especially characteristic of a presentation of symbols in apparitional form that symbol and conception resemble each other—that is, share some criterial attribute, some pattern or configuration, or, in other words, share membership in at least one class or category. An example of shared membership in such a class is: rise and fall in tension-states (a conception of inner state defined by pattern or configuration); rise and fall in melodic line or harmony (a significant or symbolic form in music); rise and fall (the class or category shared by both symbol and conception). This kind of resemblance between symbol and conception should be distinguished from imitation of a concrete particular. The main characteristic of imitation is a relative absence or low level of abstraction, an inferior conception.

Symbols in rational form are more likely to represent conceptions of entities or events that are part of external reality—that is, the reality a subject shares publicly with others. Symbols in apparitional form are more likely to represent conceptions of entities or events that are part of the inner reality of the subject—for example, conceptions of inner states involving objects imagined as internalized and the relationship between them.

The problem, especially when communication is at issue, is to create a symbol of a conception of inner reality having material existence—which is, therefore, publicly shareable—that then functions not only to represent the conception of inner reality but at least in part to exemplify it, as a particular of it, in a publicly shareable form as well. (As I discussed with you at our last meeting, not only art works but also body parts and physiological processes, actions, interactions, in fact the transference neurosis itself, may be usefully considered apparitional forms, the transference neurosis a complex one, to be sure.) In a sense, the abstract conception represented in apparitional form has its only publicly observable particular exemplification in the symbol that represents it.

Rational forms, representing conceptions that have publicly observable exemplars, may be evaluated according to the criteria of reality testing or the canons of empirical science. Apparitional forms representing conceptions that have privately observable exemplars, except for the unique exemplification embodied by the symbol itself, are evaluated according to the pleasure principle or aesthetic or appreciative criteria.

Apprehension of inner events in terms of conceptions presented in apparitional form may be manifested in an alteration in the ability of a subject or audience to discriminate aspects of inner reality and, therefore, to order or organize inner reality (e.g., Beethoven's apocryphal statement that anyone who understood his music need never be lonely again). Such power of discrimination may be manifested in an appreciation of "significant form," in an alteration in the way a subject "sees" or apprehends external reality—its significance for him —as when an audience of the works of Cézanne or Van Gogh, after appreciating such works, contemplating the conceptions represented by them, may see landscapes in the world of things-as-they-are forever differently. A work of art, insofar as it is symbolic, communicates a conception of reality, which is contemplated by its audience; it does not as a symbol merely excite its audience.

It is possible to translate from one apparitional form to another, from one rational form to another—"translation on the same level" in Pious's terms. It may be possible to translate from apparitional form to rational form, although if the conception is determined by pattern or configuration, and the only publicly observable particular exemplification of the conception is the symbol in apparitional form representing it, such a translation may be quite inadequate. For example, paraphrases of poetry are not adequate translations into another form of the conceptioi.s represented by the poem. It is possible, also, to translate from rational form to apparitional form, the limit of adequacy of such translation being determined by the extent to which and the way in which conceptions can be represented by apparitional forms. An example is the translation of latent thought by the dream-work into the manifest dream. (The converse translation is the translation of the manifest dream into rational form—the latent thought.) These translations, in Pious's terms, are "translations from one level to another."

Proto-symbolic forms are mere imitations. The more perfect the copy, the less abstraction, and, therefore, the less symbolization, is involved. The limiting case occurs when symbol, conception, and concrete, particular exemplar or referent are fused: no distinction is made between them; they are regarded as identical. For example, a word is regarded—as in schizophrenia—not as the symbol of a conception but as possessing the intrinsic efficacy of an exemplar of the conception. Apparitional forms, which represent the abstraction of significant form, pattern, or configuration, involve a higher level of symbolization. Rational forms, in general, are necessary to represent the highest levels of abstraction, and these levels of abstraction are unlikely to be achieved if rational forms are unavailable.

Shall we conclude that lower levels of consciousness are characterized by a limitation to proto-symbolic forms, and the highest levels of consciousness by the availability of rational forms?

If symbols are to be used in communication between a subject and an audience external to the subject, the resource must have material form. (This is also important even in the absence of an external audience for assuring the availability of, or supporting, the conception a symbol represents.) A symbolic medium should be easily available, easily transmitted, and should not bind its user to particular situations or contexts for use and transmission. A rare, heavy solid concentrated in one building is not useful as a medium of communication. Ideally, a medium is exchanged rather than used up in communication; its use to create symbols in one context does not set limits on its use in other contexts.

A symbolic medium, ideally, should be trivial if it is to support symbolic activity. As material object, a symbolic medium should be of little interest, importance, or significance in and of itself from the point of view of its users, and should have no special intrinsic efficacy. A trivial medium calls no attention to itself but only to the symbol for which it serves as occasion. A trivial medium is easily produced or readily available, and this accounts in part for its triviality. Paper money as a symbol of utility value and the sounds used in language are examples.

A medium that is intrinsically valuable or efficacious

is committed a priori to certain functions; it will inevitably bring about certain effects; these functions and these effects are difficult to displace by the symbolic function. If the sounds of language are felt to be intrinsically valuable or efficacious in warding off danger, winning gratification, or being in and of themselves pleasurable, their capacity to function symbolically in representing meaning may be impaired; such sounds may be pressed into service for the performance of magic instead, for example. In part, this kind of process is probably involved in what psychoanalysis formulates as the impairment of ego functioning due to failure of the neutralization of aggressive or sexual instincts, and the subordination of ego functioning to the immediate and direct gratification of the aims of such instincts.

If a medium has intrinsic meaning, especially the same meaning that is to be represented by the symbol made from it, it will be difficult to distinguish medium and symbol. In the limiting case, symbol and medium are fused; they are regarded as identical. An intrinsically valuable medium is reflective as a mirror is reflective rather than transparent. It concretely embodies value rather than serving as a vehicle for the symbolization of value. A nugget of gold or goods for barter as symbols of utility value are examples.

A medium that is not trivial is not transparent. It commands attention as an object in its own right. If an audience pays attention to the word or pigment qua sound or color, the symbol loses meaning. If an audience is distracted by the pain or excitement caused by a stimulus, if the stimulus is intrinsically and crucially gratifying or depriving, the audience is unlikely to pay any attention to its possible function as the symbol of a conception or to be free to contemplate any conception

it may be intended to represent. I include erotic excitement, and that is a comment on some contemporary
"art." In this connection, Parsons has pointed out that
"gold," which has intrinsic value, is not an ideal symbolic medium in the sense that "money" is.

An ideal symbolic medium should be particulate and
articulate. That is, a symbolic medium should have
many, clear, distinct, precisely discriminable parts,
which may be combined in an infinite variety of ways
without losing their distinct identity. The parts of a
particulate, articulate symbolic medium may be combined according to certain rules for generating meanings,
for creating symbols to represent conceptions. Gesture,
for example, is not capable of representation to the
same extent that speech is. The segments of gesture are
unclear, indistinct, and imprecisely discriminable, and
confined to combinations or relations that must occur
within the limits of a concrete space.

An ideal symbolic medium, surprisingly enough,
should be relatively inexpressive. Its expressive functions should be capable of subordination to the function
of representing conceptions. A symbolic medium cannot
be dependent upon a subject's affective states to bring it
into being (as in purely expressive utterance) or to bring
its elements into relations with one another to make a
symbol. The degree to which a symbolic medium is
bound to states that are then expressed by use of it, as
in the cries of animal "language," is inversely related to
its capacity to act as symbol. A mere expression is so
burdened with its meaning as sign that any possible
function it may have as a symbol representing conceptions tends to be overshadowed or displaced. This is
formulated in psychoanalysis as follows: instinctualiza-
tion or failure of neutralization, the urgency of the pres-

sure to achieve certain kinds of aims, is inimical at least to higher levels of symbolic functioning. The tendency of an affect such as anxiety to lose its status as a symbol (the misnomer is "signal") of a conception of a possible or future state of affairs, which may be contemplated and the contemplation of which may contribute to anticipatory action, and to become instead merely the overwhelmingly painful, disorganizing sign or expression of a present state of affairs has been well documented by psychoanalysis.

Finally, a symbol is a member of a system, a system of rules by which the parts of a symbolic medium are combined to create symbols and by which symbols are related to one another to form complex symbols. The rules for generating and combining symbols to represent meanings make the user of a symbolic medium independent of concrete, existent particulars, which need not be imitated or copied to create symbols for representing the conceptions of which such particulars are exemplars.

In summary, then, a proto-symbolic medium is constituted by private mental acts. At a higher level, a symbolic medium has material form, although it may be intrinsically valuable or efficacious, relatively indivisible and inarticulate, and primarily dependent on expressive exigencies. At the highest level of symbolization, a symbolic medium is easily available and transmitted, exchanged rather than "used up," trivial and therefore transparent, particulate and articulate, and relatively independent of expressive exigencies; its elements are combined to make symbols according to a system of rules.

May we assume that this hierarchy of symbolic medium is coordinate with a hierarchy of levels of consciousness? I confess to you that I feel consciousness to be heightened by the struggle to represent—and, therefore, both to create and to understand—a conception against the intransigence of the medium which must give the conception objective form. Our awareness of proto-symbolic forms, our private incommunicable ideas, sensations, or affects, no matter how vivid, how instantaneously keen, is transient, precarious, and difficult to recall. How swiftly the most lively dream disappears, if it is not captured in language, for example. Objectification in a symbolic form such as language—which as Cassirer has so movingly told us, is both inner and outer, material and spiritual—is necessary, if a conception is to be held and known. For such objectification skill and effort to thwart the obstinacy of the medium and the elusiveness of the conception, and the patience and consent of some audience within, are essential.

Finally, a symbolic form represents not only a subject's conceptions but at the same time inevitably—as additional aspects of its "meaning"—expresses (acts as a sign of) a subject's attitude toward his conception; his attitude toward his audience; his efforts to seize, support, and maintain his conception; and his intentions to bring about or promote certain effects. At the same time, a symbolic form may bring about effects having to do with the conception it represents; the attitudes, intentions, and effort of which it is a sign; its own intrinsic—that is, nonsymbolic—efficacy as an object in and of itself; and the characteristics of the audience upon which it impinges.

We are already touching—and I have only the time and strength merely to touch—upon another difficult topic in the realm of symbolic process: the status of affect. (Many of you have become, I know, restless at my emphasis upon conception, mistaking it for overvaluation of the merely intellectual; I remind you of the various ways Freud used the term "idea.") Affect may be a sign of the attitude of the symbolizer to his conception, an index of the quality and intensity of the value he attributes to it with regard to his own interests, wishes, intentions. Affect may also—a subtle but important difference—be a form used to symbolize a conception of a state of affairs by its begetter. More complexly still, an affect may symbolize his conception of the inner or outer audience to whom the symbol is presented. Affect appears to function as well to mobilize energies to overcome obstacles to the creation and maintenance of the symbolic representation of the conception and to carry out the intention that presentation of the symbolic form is designed to serve. But, for now, enough of such mysteries.

Let me conclude this overlong discussion by suggesting that crucial aspects of the capacity to achieve, maintain, or regain higher levels of symbolization activity— and therefore, may I assert, higher levels of consciousness—include, then, at least the availability of controls for modulating, mitigating, and in various ways managing the expressive aspects of a symbolic form, which may otherwise disturb its function as the representation of a conception. They include also the skill and effort required to struggle against the intransigent medium and to capture the evasive conception; and the patience and consent of the audience for whom the symbolic form is created, especially the audience within onself.

I am surprised to see some of you still here, after this long, somewhat strained, and exceedingly dry presentation. I am exhausted, and I am sure you must be, too. I shall stop now with the firm resolve to leave these arid regions, to recount to you when next we meet some of my experiences in the treatment of mental illness, and then to consider with you the application of some of these ideas to those experiences.

4: The Treatment of a Mental Illness

Ladies and gentlemen:

I would not be surprised if we were lucky enough to have in this auditorium the makings of a model of the idea of a mental illness we have been exploring—and without LSD! For notice: you are trying to achieve and maintain a level of functioning at which my comments will make some sense to you. What interferes?

For one of you, something about me or my performance interferes. You feel a gap between us. I am lost in these pages. I do not look at you. Perhaps you feel I do not care whether you understand me or not. You try in vain to catch my eye and when it does not fall upon you, you have a vague, disagreeable sense of being invisible. You give up. Your mind wanders. You fall into reverie. You catch a glimpse of my mouth, which seems unusually large, my teeth unusually long and sharp—only for an instant. You shake yourself to make that impression go away, distracting yourself immediately by checking your memory of an interesting equation you came across recently.

For another of you, something about your body interferes. Perhaps you have a cold; your chest is tight; your head aches; you slept poorly. Perhaps you studied or made love far into the night. You are exhausted. It is all you can do to keep your eyes open. Not that you do not wish to arouse yourself, to awaken, to attend, but the capacities upon which you call seem limited and feeble. Your eyelids fall. You startle at the strange, loud sound of my voice. You are momentarily confused. What is he saying? What does that single word, hanging there in peculiar isolation, mean? Your eyelids fall again.

One of you may welcome this hour as a respite from the demands of some personal relationship to which you have devoted yourself. Tears have fallen and you have given comfort. You have listened and answered questions. You have responded to the insistent longing in a touch even as the touch was supposedly given, a gift, to you. You have seen the intense look and returned one as intense. You have spent hours together. You want to be quiet now, and even as you try to meet my thought with your own, you are distracted by memories of another and by the desire even for an hour to think of no one at all.

Perhaps one of you received news on your way to this auditorium that startled or frightened you, or perhaps as you drove here, your mind on something else, another car, suddenly, out of nowhere, swerved toward you, almost hitting your car, leaving you with a painful, clear realization that you could easily have been killed. For a moment you felt you had been killed. You struggled to pull yourself together, to ignore the shock; you may have tried to kid yourself out of a mood. But now, dazed and empty, you have difficulty concentrating.

Another of you perhaps struggles with the wish to be here and the wish not to be here at all, the wish to listen and the angry wish to silence me, the wish to be and the wish not to be a physician. You are reminded unpleasantly of your father who loved to get the family together so that he might read aloud. You could not sit still; you tried to steal from the room to go to the bathroom; and you remember the terror and anger you felt when he suddenly lashed out with his loud angry voice and you burst into tears—all the more painful that you felt his bafflement and pitied him as well. You have committed your forces to one stalemated engagement after another. Like a battle-weary soldier, you peer through a miasma of anxiety, constantly alert to nameless dangers. You consider yourself lucky to get through the lecture without bolting and you may help yourself to sit through it by carefully writing down, with as much order as possible, something of what you hear me say, just as I steer myself through it with the aid of this rostrum and the notes before me.

You notice that I have chosen to read from these pages rather than to speak extemporaneously. That choice, I think, is my hedge against the following imagined experience. I stand before you. In the midst of speaking, I see you. I look at your faces and they are still. Suddenly, I feel my mind go blank, my tongue grow heavy and halt. These pages, to which I may seem to cling as a falling man clings to a rope, ensure me the presence of an audience to whom I can speak.

Certainly, each of you has had the experience to which I now refer. Like me, you have gone to an interview, keyed up, excited, feeling that you started off with élan, the words rushing to your tongue lightly, eagerly, with verve and intelligence. You look at the interviewer. His face is silent, cold, unsympathetic, and unresponsive. Perhaps quite suddenly, your mind goes blank. The words will not come. Your force yourself to speak—a great deal depends on your doing so. The words come now only with difficulty; they are heavy, sound stupid. You can just about get them out; they sound like the words of someone else. Unutterably weary, you sigh with relief when the interview is over, and feel restored to yourself.

I thought again of this kind of experience, preparing these lectures. When I started writing, I conjured up in my mind's eye an ideal audience. Every line I wrote was received with just the sympathy, the smile, the friendly twinkle, the understanding, the rush of pleasure it called for. With each such response from that ideal student and colleague in my mind the words came rushing with exhilaration to my pen.

Then I spoke to you some weeks ago. Despite my efforts to insulate myself from the reality of your response, word reached me of it. Instead of one ideal companion of the intellect, I was forced to become aware of all the different "you's" out there, with different backgrounds, needs, preferences, speaking different languages (not all of them mine and mine a stranger to many) and suffering different anxieties. No *one* with whom I could speak—and if I chose any with whom to speak, I now watched with my mind's eye another turn away.

The preparation of the next lecture was much more difficult than that of the previous ones, went more slowly, and took more effort. You will agree that the strain was expressed in the very form of the lecture. Some element of that strain I blame on the effort I was forced to exert to reconstitute painfully the image of my companion of the intellect in my mind, so that I could speak again.

I do not think this experience much different from the difficulty the schizophrenic patient has in retaining from one session to another an image of the psychotherapist in his mind to whom he can speak. Following each session, this image slips away, is damaged, is distorted. Over and over again, this image must be recovered and repaired if the patient is to return and, returning, be able to speak again with the psychotherapist.

As a matter of fact, changes in the representation of the therapist are important to an understanding of the process of psychotherapy with any patient, no matter what the nature of his illness. Changes in the internalized image of the therapist determine much that is puzzling in psychotherapy—inexplicable and often abrupt alterations in ambience from one session to another; sudden difficulties in communication—and are important in evaluating the direction and outcome of psychotherapy. Similar problems (the mystery of creativity; the vicissitudes of, including inhibitions or blocks in, creative work) are also clarified by reference to changes in images of listening or looking objects imagined within or—of ultimate significance in both creative work and mental illness—in images of the self as listener or looker. Ultimately, it is from the self in its function as superego that the creative worker receives permission to carry out one intention rather than another, to wait for a conception to realize itself, to move from one type of symbolic process to another, to pass freely from one level of organization or consciousness to another. The self imagined by the schizophrenic patient offers no similar consent. It is this difference that makes the creative worker in his functioning relatively independent of actual interpersonal relations, and the schizophrenic patient in his functioning, despite his apparent aloofness, so dependent upon and reactive to them.

Can we avoid succumbing either to a shallow environmentalism, with its wishful optimism, or a fatalistic physicalism with its invitation to operate upon the patient as object? Is not the aim of psychotherapy to enable the patient to beget a new self-representation, not simply by providing him with beneficent "interpersonal experiences" that teach him an altered conception of himself, but by requiring him to articulate, to form, to use new materials in representing, his self-conception so that in giving it new shape at a higher level of consciousness he both discovers and creates it? One difficulty with Freud's early notion of "the Unconscious" as a system, particularly in conjunction with his archaeological metaphors, was the implication that conceptions lie finished but buried in that system waiting to be dug up, rather than—as Freud's metaphor of the patient in psychoanalysis who is a sculptor uncovering the self that waits to be revealed in marble stone instead implies— that conceptions of self are discovered through their creation, in the medium not of marble but, for example, first of the materials of the transference neurosis, and, ultimately, of language. This process begins when in treatment the patient is required to symbolize the conceptions represented by his symptoms in another medium.

But I have taken another detour into speculation. Let us return to imagining the schizophrenic patient experiencing such states as these you and I have experienced here, not for brief moments, but over and over and for long periods of time. Imagine even greater drops in level of functioning, occurring perhaps with catastrophic suddenness. Imagine such a patient attempting, slowly, painfully, with diminished capacity, to recover from such losses of level, only to fall back repeatedly, because he is even more vulnerable to such losses of level at lower levels of functioning, losing hope, losing confidence that recovery can ever be achieved or, once achieved, that it can be maintained.

Almost immediately after preparing this lecture, I came across an allusion to the 19th Freud Anniversary Lecture of the New York Pyschoanalytic Institute by Charles Fisher, who reports research purporting to make the astonishing discovery that nightmares do not occur during REM sleep (a stage of light sleep associated with ordinary dreaming, from which it is relatively easy to awaken). Nightmares occur rather during the three stages of successively deeper sleep, and stage four, the period of deepest sleep, is also the period of the most severe nightmares. The nightmare is described as a massive failure of ego functioning, from which the subject awakens with a bloodcurdling scream, dissociated, confused, hallucinating, and unresponsive to the environment. Perhaps, then, our statement that the schizophrenic patient falls precipitously, catastrophically, from one level of functioning to another, into an abyss, and that many of his symptoms manifest his struggle to awaken from a nightmare in which he feels trapped, is more than a mere figure of speech.

All of us have some knowledge of nightmares. In looking at our own experience in this auditorium, we have touched, though ever so lightly, upon the elements of psychosis. I want to emphasize that the schizophrenic person has no experience of which we are incapable. Perhaps his functioning is more precarious, more susceptible to prolonged, disastrous interruption, than yours or mine, but he knows nothing that we are forever deprived of understanding. That we are more efficient than he in guarding against such interruptions and recovering from them is certainly useful to us in many situations, although it is not an unmixed blessing when it comes to our attempts to treat schizophrenic persons. Then, our zeal and efficiency in protecting ourselves from such states as we have glimpsed in this hour may work to separate us from the schizophrenic person for whom we care. We cannot tolerate him as a man, in part because of the possibilities of which he reminds us in ourselves. So he must become a thing upon which we operate. In your professional careers, you will have to judge for yourselves when assertions of the certainty of an organic defect in schizophrenia are essentially assertions that nothing so strange can be related to experience as you or I know it. I regret to inform you that decisions to treat the physiological organism with electricity or drugs too often, it seems to me, involve the effort to ignore or suppress symbolizations (not necessarily verbal) of states we physicians cannot stand. In psychotherapy, we psychotherapists may withdraw—I use the word advisedly—into a professional role, replete with diagnostic and psychodynamic terms: just listen to the average case presentation! A psychotherapist may offer pontifical "interpretations"—the very word may be used in a way to suggest his distance from his patient —while the therapist, of course, at the same time attributes the untoward effects of such interpretations to the inability of the schizophrenic patient to make use of psychotherapy aiming at insight because of a "defective" ego. In the same way, the psychotherapist may bestow kindly forbearance, indulgence, and the ubiquitous "management," as if he were training a benighted member of a subhuman species.

Do you remember the emphasis in the first conception of schizophrenia on the narcissism of the schizophrenic person, his self-absorption, his withdrawal from others? I urge you to observe for yourselves, paying careful attention to the subtle nuances by which one person indicates he has removed himself from another, when a psychotherapist, family member, nurse, or friend complains of that notorious difficulty in maintaining a relationship with a schizophrenic person: who, in fact, withdraws from whom?

Ladies and gentlemen, I know that one question is the most important to you. Do our conceptions of schizophrenia, for example, in fact help us to care for the schizophrenic person? Of course, I would like to convince you—I am always engaged in the effort to convince myself—that psychotherapeutic treatment in psychiatry has some elements of rationality; that is, that at the least our care of the patient bears some meaningful relation to our conception of what ails him. Ideally, we should be able to demonstrate that the psychotherapy of schizophrenia addresses itself to the elimination of the etiologic or pathogenic event, to the mitigation of the morbid process, or to the support of the reparative efforts that are the personality system's own response to the morbid process. As you will already have anticipated, I am going to wander about a bit during this lecture, but what guides me through the maze of my own thoughts is the effort to clarify the state of affairs we conceive as schizophrenia, the state of affairs we wish to bring about through psychotherapy, and in what ways psychotherapy is an adequate means to transform one state of affairs into the other.

Those of you who have not worked with a schizophrenic patient, imagine you face your first such patient. He walks with a curious mixture of diffidence and arrogance into the emergency room, the examining room, your office. He is wearing a heavy jacket, which he does not remove when he sits down. He glances at you, looks away; he may smile to himself; you have a fleeting and hardly comfortable impression that he knows something he is not telling. He says nothing. Now what? You are about to say something. What will you say? What will happen between the two of you during that first meeting?

Perhaps you comfort yourself that in such an inexact field, involving such gross transactions, you are permitted a wide margin of error. I have been haunted from time to time by the conviction that clumsiness in symbolic activity, such as psychotherapy involves, is as fateful for the future of treatment as the slip of a surgeon's knife. That suggests we should know at least as much about ourselves as symbolizing beings, about the meanings of what we express and how we express such meanings, as the surgeon knows about his hand and knife. But perhaps you feel, as I sometimes do in moments of fatigue, that it is unfair to expect us physicians, who have spent most of our waking lives learning to manipulate things, to become as sensitive, precise, and scrupulous in the use of word and gesture as a poet must be, for whose enterprise the placement of a syllable is fateful. I would not blame you if in the face of such exacting requirements you forsake such work forever for the pill and the knife.

Nevertheless, we are here today to consider that other tool with which you may confront your patient's illness —psychotherapy. As a psychotherapist, your job, most simply, is to understand this person who sits silently facing you and to communicate in ways that are meaningful to him your attempts to understand. What do I mean by "understand"? That would take us many hours to discuss. Provisionally, let us agree that if you understand your patient, minimally, you are able from moment to moment to see—by which I mean both think and feel—the world as he conceives it to be and himself as he conceives himself to be. That presupposes you are able to translate the language—not necessarily verbal—in which he wittingly or unwittingly, with various degrees of consciousness, represents these conceptions. More ambitiously, perhaps, eventually, you might even be able to formulate with him some ideas to explain how these representations of the world and self come to have the shape and content they do have and change in the ways they do change.

More formally, I would define psychotherapy as treatment by symbolic means, directed to the personality system; the personality system is constituted by symbolic processes. Psychotherapy is applicable to the elimination of etiologic or pathogenic events, the mitigation of morbid processes, or the support of reparative efforts, when such events, processes, or efforts are constituted by symbolization or its impairment.

The nature, extent, and duration of the effects a psychotherapeutic endeavor may be expected to have probably depends in part upon the extent to which it involves control of the conditions in which vicissitudes of symbolization are to occur and be observed. These conditions are especially those in which symbolization processes emerge that either in form or in content under other conditions do not make themselves readily available. I am speaking now of the degree of sophistication or discipline evident in the use of a treatment modality; what I say has analogies in every medical discipline.

Psychotherapy should be distinguished from treatment methods making use of nonsymbolic agents, for example, surgical interventions, drugs, and so on, to the extent that these are regarded as intrinsically rather than symbolically efficacious. Psychotherapy should also be distinguished from treatment methods directed to other than personality systems (even when these methods involve talking)—for example, those considered to have their principal impact upon the physiological organism (we might refer to physiological therapy) or upon such social or interactional systems as the family, other small groups, a hospital community, a neighborhood community, city, or some other portion of society (we might refer to sociotherapy, which encompasses then such enterprises as family therapy, therapy of the group, milieu therapy, and community therapy).

As I have already said in other words, a psychotherapist seeks to understand the symbolizations of his patient, in both their aspects as suasive messages or communications to the psychotherapist and their aspects as representations of conceptions of the patient's world and self. The psychotherapist seeks to respond to his patient's symbolizations in ways that symbolize and communicate his understanding of them to the patient. The psychotherapist's skill is also called upon to control conditions that will either enhance or support these processes, on the one hand, or limit, constrain, or interfere with them, on the other.

What is the therapeutic action of such activities by the psychotherapist? Whatever it is, I am not inclined for reasons that must be apparent to you to believe that it can be described in terms appropriate to the rewiring of tangled circuits or that it involves extinguishing the effects of previous automatic stimulus-response conditioning and substituting for such effects the linkage of new reactions to signals.

Would you think it quixotic of me to regard psychotherapy as a process of becoming more fully awake? I realize that I may sacrifice what respect you have left for psychotherapy as an enterprise, if I seem to say that the psychotherapist is essentially, not merely metaphorically, enabling the patient to awaken. But I cannot help that. Psychotherapy is a process of becoming more fully awake. Psychotherapy is a process that increases the capacity of its participants—perhaps, we should say "both participants"—to attain voluntarily a state of becoming more fully awake. I like that way of putting it very much.

I am sure, however, that some of you regard such a formulation with puzzlement, if not skeptical mockery. I wonder as I think about your puzzlement and your skepticism if we do not underestimate the extent to which becoming able to speak the unspoken or unspeakable makes possible a higher level of functioning or organization to the personality system.

May I remind you of a passage from Helen Keller's autobiography, quoted for similar reasons in that excellent work of Susanne Langer's, *Philosophy in a New Key*? Miss Keller records the passage from a world of signs to a world of symbolic activity, made possible by the advent of language. "[My teacher] brought me my hat, and I knew I was going out into the warm sunshine." That is an example of life in a world of signs. "This thought, if a wordless sensation may be called a thought, made me hop and skip with pleasure." It is clear that Miss Keller doubts that symbolic activity, that thought, may occur without language, some sort of language, that is more than sign, that is in fact symbolization. Contrast that view with Sullivan's notion that language is but "grace notes" upon thought.

The passage continues:

We walked down the path to the well-house, attracted by the fragrance of the honeysuckle with which it was covered. Some one was drawing water and my teacher placed my hand under the spout. As the cool stream gushed over my hand she spelled into the other the word *water,* first slowly, then rapidly. I stood still, my whole attention fixed upon the motion of her fingers. Suddenly I felt a misty consciousness as of something forgotten—a thrill of returning thought; and somehow the mystery of language was revealed to me. I knew then that w-a-t-e-r meant the wonderful cool something that was flowing over my hand. That living word awakened my soul, gave it light, hope, joy, set it free! There were barriers still, it is true, but barriers that in time could be swept away.

I left the well-house eager to learn. Everything had a name, and each name gave birth to a new thought. As we returned to the house every object which I touched seemed to quiver with life. That was because I saw everything with the strange, new sight that had come to me.

I think that what is happening in this description, and what happens in psychotherapy, not only in response to particular interpretations but in response to the process itself, bear a profound resemblance, although I do not yet have the theoretical tools to articulate what it is.

Incidentally, I am reminded of the criticism of some of you and others of many psychiatrists for their interest in psychotherapy as a treatment modality, not only on the grounds of difficulties in making psychotherapy widely available or of our own inadequacies as psychotherapists in symbolizing and communicating with those carrying on these activities in ways different from ourselves, but rather on the grounds that psychotherapy is culturally appropriate to the verbal middle-class but inapplicable to members of the so-called lower socio-economic class who, so it is claimed, do not value words. For them, then, pills and advice.

I wonder if it does not occur to such critics that a scarcity of language resources is not simply a preferred life style but rather a serious handicap in living, and that an inability to symbolize emotional, physiological, and sensory experience is not incidental to psychological illness but may in fact doom an individual to it. When we psychiatrists are exhorted to use other culturally more appropriate methods than psychotherapy in treating the lower socioeconomic class citizen—to accept, to adjust, so to speak, to his level of functioning—are we being asked to abandon him to a life of sleepwalking in a twilight zone of quasi-consciousness, in which he must depend for relief of his pain solely upon the efficient manipulation of his body and his environment? (The same objections, of course, have been raised about psychotherapy with the inarticulate adolescent, with the impulse-ridden patient who does rather than talks, with the schizophrenic person who supposedly cannot and does not want to communicate.)

Actually, of course, if you decide that the etiologic or pathogenic event is a frustration arising from obstacles to the patient's actualization of some conception of the desirable, and if you decide that a major obstacle is the recalcitrance of the object world, you may set about attempting to alter this unfavorable situation in which the patient finds himself. You may recommend that he enter a hospital, in hopes that he will find there a less inimical, a more congenial, milieu than that in which he finds himself. You may advise him to leave home, to enroll in school or to drop out of school, to divorce his wife, or to change his job. You may meet the patient together with his parents, siblings, wife, or children, seeking to modify these others or rather the system of interactions involving them all.

That I do not call such measures—directed to the object world—psychotherapy follows from my definition of psychotherapy. That such measures may be useful under particular circumstances (and the ability to recognize such circumstances is part of clinical skill) no one can deny who is willing to acknowledge that nonsymbolic aspects of reality—that is, the conditions in which we exert effort to achieve ends—play a part in determining the outcome of such efforts. However, for the most part, in my experience such measures even when useful fall far short of what is required.

The main reason for this is, of course, that the object world that constitutes the obstacle is the object world as the patient conceives it to be, his symbolic representations of it. Our manipulations of the object world do not necessarily affect his conceptions of it. A situation may be changed or he may be removed from it, but he carries his symbolic representations of reality and the processes by which these are created with him wherever he goes. When the patient says, as patients have often said to me, "My mother is inside me," he means just that. He is not using a mere figure of speech. The object-representation of his mother to which he refers is inside him, part of him; it was formed long ago by a being that he was and is in some sense no longer; but it is still inside him and remains inside him whether the tired, old lady whom he recognizes as mother now resembles it or not. We may induce him to pity this tired, old lady, if he does not already do so, by talking with them together, but that alone will not change his relation to the terrifying, seductive image to which he is so attached or his propensity for conjuring it up again and again.

Now, by none of this do I mean to deny, for example, that the family life of the schizophrenic patient has actually been extraordinarily unpleasant and literally maddening. In fact, once I have acquired not a cursory but over months a detailed knowledge of a schizophrenic patient's family life, of the kind Lidz and his colleagues have reported, I have never had any difficulty understanding why the patient is schizophrenic, never felt that under the circumstances, given who he was and who his parents were and who their parents were, he could have been other than schizophrenic, never felt called upon to postulate an organic defect to make explicable how anyone raised in such a home in such ways could possibly have become schizophrenic. My usual feeling, in fact, upon acquiring such knowledge has been to regard the alternative we call schizophrenia as probably the only one possible to the patient if he was to survive at all and even sometimes as the best of a number of dismal, and even hideous, other possibilities conceivably available to him. I have usually been moved to congratulate him in my mind for the feat of managing as well as he had. As a physician, as a psychiatrist, and perhaps—I do not know—especially as a Jew, I respect man's capacity to survive. Though the misshapen forms of his survival—the distracted, warped, and constricted self—may make us wince, may make us cry, may repel us, they also command respect.

I once had a patient who told me for many months with great rage of the father who persecuted him, who hated him, interfered with him, whose eye was always upon him. Everywhere he went, there that eye pursued him with its malevolent, watchful stare. That this con-

ception of his father seemed to bear little resemblance
to the worried and seemingly far from frightening old
man who came to visit him in the hospital certainly
bothered the patient. I suppose in part this discrepancy
between the reality he recognized and the reality he felt
led him to conclude, often with considerable despair,
how crazy he must be. Fortunately, I did not suffer
from the belief that I had good sense, that he did not,
that I was in touch with reality, that he was not, or that
I had a duty to impart my good sense to him and,
therefore, to rub his nose in the discrepancy that already moved him to despair.

During many months many things happened between
us and within him. At first he lived in nightmare most of
the time. Then he began to tell me of dreams, which is
perhaps to say that gradually there came a time when he
slept and dreamt during the night and was awake at least
some of the day. He dreamt of going fishing—he and his
father had fished together—and gradually the representations of fishing in his dreams changed from sinking boat,
churning waves, and sea monsters to voyages in which
by his father's side he took the wheel and steered the
boat. That change was a change in *his* object world—in
the object-representations and self-representations of
inner reality, in a reality symbolically created, in psychic reality, in the reality in which we are all so im-
mersed we only dimly perceive from time to time that it
is there and that it is in that reality we live.

Then my patient told me that when he was a boy he
had spent many months in bed with a life-endangering
illness. Now he remembered vividly how his father, apparently upon a physician's instructions, restricted his
activity, and how his father came often in the night to
see him, to check the windows and his covers, to look

upon him, to make sure he was all right—and the feelings stirred in him by these experiences. It would have taken a particular act of imagination and some experience, which I did not then have, to be able to hear and see this father and this boy in the raging patient and the image of the persecuting, angry, intruding eye. Yet they were there and a psychotherapist can wait, at least, for months if necessary, until the meaning of a patient's representations becomes clear.

This patient eventually helped me to understand that he had felt persecuted by love, and that as he had felt love to be dangerous to him—this had something to do with his mother, too, of course—so he felt his own love to be dangerous to others. It was then perhaps, although I did not realize it until later, that I began to have doubts about the formulation that the essential morbid process in schizophrenia is a narcissistic regression or hypercathexis of the self. It was also then perhaps that I began to think that a delusion may not be simply the creation of a false reality, substituted for a painful true reality in the interests of gratification, but rather might involve the patient's use of a particular, and for most of us peculiar, kind of language to represent, think over, and communicate certain conceptions he has of his object world, self, and his past experience.

May those of you who are beginning your work as psychotherapists have the luck I had—to find and be taught by a patient who is willing to teach you and from whom you are willing to learn.

There is another way you may set about attempting to alter this unfavorable object world in which the patient finds himself. You may decide to make up for its deficiencies yourself, and to provide the patient with opportunities for gratification in the relationship with you.

Such strategies of treatment are sometimes rationalized by a belief in corrective emotional experience as the essential therapeutic ingredient of psychotherapy.

I am at a loss as to how to comment on this matter within this short lecture and with the conceptual tools we have developed so far.

Let us dispose immediately of this position when it rests simply upon the failure to recognize that it is inner or symbolically created reality with which we are concerned and that this reality, by the time we come face to face with the patient, is not necessarily and not even usually altered simply by the presence of opportunities for gratification.

That the quality of the relationship between psychotherapist and patient is crucial for changes in the patient's capacity to symbolize and to achieve higher levels of organization and functioning and for changes in the form and content of his conceptions of himself and others I have no doubt. That this quality has anything to do with the psychotherapist's intention to make up for deficiencies in the patient's life or to provide him with opportunities for gratification in the therapeutic relationship I very much doubt.

I once was grandiose enough to offer something like that in the way, I thought, of comfort in a trying time and the patient about whom I have spoken to you let me know immediately and unmistakably, with more anger than I usually care to be exposed to, that treating someone like a child who can be distracted from grief with "candy" is insulting as well as useless.

I would have thought that if there is anything I have learned from this patient, and from others as well, it is that "you can't go home again," and that, in the words of the song, "you've got to cross that lonely valley by yourself." It is certainly possible to recognize a patient's pain and to let him know you recognize it: that is a great deal! It is not necessary to try to make the pain go away or to promise that it will. In fact, nothing is so destructive to a relationship with a patient as the implicit or explicit communication, in words or actions, of promises that can never be kept. There is no way to make up to a patient for anything he has missed or that he misses. There is no starting all over again and giving the patient the childhood, or being the mother or father, you or he phantasy he should have had.

Yet I am troubled about saying any of this to you because the matter is so complex that I am sure I have said something in these few words that can be easily misunderstood. I am also troubled because some of my own teachers, whose clinical and personal wisdom I respect, sometimes seem to me to be saying that there can be a new beginning for a patient in psychotherapy, that he can find in this relationship what he missed as an infant, that it is possible to go home again. It is likely I have misunderstood them. Or perhaps there is something in all this that future patients will help me to understand better.

To come back to your patient. I think it may matter a great deal to the future of your work with him whether you regard the morbid process in which he is entangled as, on the one hand, a narcissistic regression, a hypercathexis of the self, in response to frustration, or, on the other hand, an impoverishment or depletion of the capacity of the personality system to achieve, to maintain, or, having lost it, to regain a higher level of organization or functioning, in response to the impact of an object world that does not support symbolization processes.

I think we have to be careful how we characterize this

object world. It is not, I think, an adequate formulation to say that the schizophrenic person has not learned to be rational or, conversely, has learned to be irrational in experiences with the object world. A few sessions with your schizophrenic patient may convince you that these formulations are inadequate. He might astonish and perplex you by coming in one day with eyes alight and clear voice to discuss relations between the characters and issues in the works, say, of Dostoevsky and Conrad, or, for that matter, the relations between his parents or between them and him or between you and him, with a degree of subtlety, cogency, articulateness, and insight you would be hard put to discover in your colleagues; perhaps the very next day he will stare at you blankly, yawn, mutter, and, with a poverty of language that is remarkable given the sophisticated vocabulary of yesterday, struggle to put the simplest words together. It is as if both of you peer at each other through a glass darkly; the inordinate sense of effort that you will experience at such moments even to see your patient, and I mean this literally, unclouded and without perceptual distortions, much less to keep on talking with him is, in my experience, pathognomonic of the presence of schizophrenia.

It is the stability of higher level functioning that is at issue, not merely its presence or absence. The patient does not have the same success we do in passing from one level of functioning to another, up or down, voluntarily, and according to changes in the demands on him. His drops in level are relatively abrupt and catastrophic in extent; and they are experienced by him as outside his voluntary control—thus, the uncanniness and terror of schizophrenic states. Prolonged effort must be expended to recover from such drops. Such efforts at recovery—which we often have difficulty recognizing as such in the symptomatology, behavior, and communications of the schizophrenic person—are precariously maintained, yielding with relative ease upon impact with new drops in level of functioning. Different forms of schizophrenia are probably related, then, to the forms that such efforts at recovery take, the amount and persistence of the effort, and the degree and stability of the success achieved.

What is the contribution of the object world to this state of affairs?

The object world may not provide resources or incentives required for higher level organization or functioning or it may be, in a variety of ways, positively disruptive of such higher level organization or functioning.

Symbolization may be disrupted by drastic, abrupt, confusing, distracting, or excessive intrusions. Demands for higher level symbolization may exceed the innate and acquired capacities of the schizophrenic person or may exceed the effort that is available for higher level symbolization, or that can be allocated to it, given the variety or magnitude of demands upon him. (If this be your conception of the patient's state of affairs, you would not necessarily want to lure or urge your already overtaxed patient to engage in interpersonal relations as though you believed that the main difficulty is that he has turned from interpersonal relations to an excessive preoccupation with himself.)

The object world may fail to encourage, support, or reward the effort to achieve or sustain higher levels of functioning. Since symbolization processes are significantly future-oriented, persistent disappointment or the thwarting of expectations may lead to the conviction that it is futile to expend effort in achieving higher levels of symbolization. (We may remember here that three of the subsystems of personality—the symbolic processes of which are differentiated from id-processes by just this characteristic—require some conception of, orientation to, and attitude toward the future: ego-ideal processes function to recreate the past in the future; ego processes function to create the present for the sake of the future; and superego processes function to create the future out of the possibilities of the present.)

You will, I think, be impressed by your patient's sense of futility. He may describe this as depression, but it is important for you to realize that he means he is without hope. (Incidentally, if one of you is interested in carrying out a simple investigation, I suggest you examine the use of the future tense by schizophrenic patients. Presumably, it may make a difference to thought if reference to the future is altered or absent from the thinker's frame of reference. In this connection, it is suggestive that Whorf, for example, holds that the Hopis' world view is different from ours, since their language refers to validity or the grounds for assertion when our language refers to time or temporal sequence.)

For most of us, rational thought, which is concerned with the relation of means to ends, presupposes a hopeful orientation to the future, that we care about ends we want and expect to attain. Such hopes and expectations have usually been persistently disappointed in the life of the schizophrenic person. If this is so, it follows that the restoration of hope in relationship with the psychotherapist, for example, should result in an apparent improvement in the ability to think logically; I believe I have seen something like that. It also follows that disappointment in the relationship with the psychotherapist may result in an apparent impairment or perhaps lack of interest in the ability to think logically; I believe I have seen that too.

Another way of looking at this matter is that the schizophrenic person is not primarily concerned in his thought and symbolization with the relation of means to ends, but rather with an attempt to create or discover meaningful ends. He may be seeking in his symbolization to establish some sense of solidarity with the object world, to feel himself related to it in meaningful ways, so that he can imagine gratifying end states of affairs he might seek to bring into being and maintain. A different level of symbolization from that involved in rational thought or logical discourse may be functional for the attempt to endow ends with cathexis or value—more like the symbolization in myth, art, or religion. You may miss the point if you hear a patient's communication primarily in terms of its rationality. Rationality may be beside the point; the patient is up to something else in his communications—perhaps an attempt to establish some kind of union or continuity with you, or a bond between you and him.

Finally, the object world may be of such a nature that symbolization processes are not valued. Nothing about the object world directs attention to them or invests them with value. Federn has pointed out that focusing the schizophrenic patient's attention upon his ego states and ego functions, upon symbolization processes and when and how these occur, in painstaking detail, tends to improve ego functioning or, as we might say, raise the level of functioning at which symbolization occurs. One must be interested in the details of how the patient sees and feels himself and the world, and how, under what circumstances and in what sequence exactly, changes in such states and conceptions occur. As you show such interest, the patient may become interested; as he becomes interested, he begins to symbolize at a higher level.

The degree of impact of such an object world depends upon the extent to which it impinges upon an already relatively unstable system of symbolic processes, including always both object-representations and self-representations.

Suppose you meet your patient a few times. He begins to call you between sessions or to send messages to you. Disaster is imminent. He has failed in this. He has failed in that. He cannot cope. He will never be able to cope. He must have medication. He cannot stay out of a hospital. (If he is in a hospital: he cannot get out of the hospital.) It is hopeless. He is helpless. He is overwhelmed. He provides you with material. You make interpretations. You and he see how he takes revenge on his family, perhaps how he treats you as a member of the family. The interpretations have no effect. You encourage him. Complications in his life pile up, one thing leading to another in a downward spiral apparently nothing can stop. He will kill himself. You must do something. Under these circumstances, you may try to do something. Whatever it is, it doesn't work. You try to do something else. It doesn't work. You are increasingly anxious about him. You feel harried. The patient is getting more incoherent. You wonder if treatment with this patient is going to get anywhere. You begin to consider electroshock or the state hospital or transfer to another psychotherapist.

Suppose you do not respond by doing something. Suppose instead something like this happens. The patient comes in. He looks at you. He says, "You look

angry." You say, meaning it, "I am." He, much surprised, asks, "Why?" You say, meaning it, "The way
you keep after me, intruding upon me, pressing me—you
push me and push me and push me—until I can't think. I
don't like not being able to think." He says, "It's funny
you should say that. That's just the way I've been feeling. My parents put so much pressure on me to do well
at school, it gets so bad, I can't think."

You realize with some surprise that the tone of voice
in which he says this, the clarity and thoughtfulness of
it, mean that you have actually translated at last what
he has been trying to communicate in his language, and
that this translation has made possible a higher level of
functioning to him. You ponder about the level of symbolization at which he arouses feelings in you as a way
of representing what he feels. Perhaps you think about
dreams, and how he might assign feelings to a figure in a
dream to represent a meaning in that dream. But that
means—you are uncomfortable when this occurs to you
—that in a sense you have been a character in a kind of
dream of his.

Suppose at another time the patient begins to miss
appointments. When you can, you make interpretations
concerning his avoidance and perhaps what he tries to
avoid. He agrees. He continues to miss appointments. If
he is an inpatient, you send the nurse to get him. He
comes late. He will only come if you send the nurse to
get him. You begin to get fed up with that. You issue an
ultimatum: you will no longer send for him. If he
doesn't come on his own, he will have to miss appointments. He doesn't come on his own. Or, if he is an
outpatient, you call him on the telephone. He does not
answer. Next time he sees you, he tells you he was
there; he knew it was you when the telephone rang; he

did not want to answer. You think to yourself that
schizophrenic patients are narcissistic and that it is impossible to establish a relationship with them. You wonder if treatment with this patient is going to get anywhere. You begin to consider electroshock or the state
hospital or transfer to another psychotherapist.

Suppose you do not respond by doing something.
Suppose instead something like this happens. He says,
"I'm too afraid to come to the appointments, I feel
you're angry at me." You do not reassure him. You say,
somewhat snappishly, "So what if I am angry, or if you
are, for that matter. That doesn't mean we have to
break up." He says, "It's funny you should say that. I've
been worried that since I missed these appointments,
maybe it's no use and we should stop meeting." You
say, suddenly remembering a wish he expressed somewhat casually some time ago to see more of you, "Maybe it would be a good idea, if we can work it out, to
have another appointment during the week. I think you
could use it." He says, sounding relieved, "I think I
could." He asks if he can make up the appointment he
has just missed. You make another appointment with
him. He begins to attend sessions regularly and on time.
You ponder what it means that a patient who wants to
see you more often communicates this by a representation of it in its opposite—coming less often—just as a
meaning might be represented through primary process
by its opposite in a dream.

The schizophrenic person often functions at a level of
symbolization where the materials that he uses to represent and communicate include, as in a dream, actions,
body parts and sensations, and the eliciting of feelings in
the psychotherapist. As in a dream, he represents meanings by their opposites and condenses many meanings in

one representation. I think it is possible that the grandiosity of the schizophrenic person may be understood as such a representation, rather than simply as a manifestation of his infatuation with himself.

Characteristically, in work with schizophrenic patients, the psychotherapist finds himself invaded by strangely intense affects—moved in subtle ways, apparently by the patient, to respond in ways that are disagreeably alien to the psychotherapist's usual notions about himself. Many times, these feelings and alien conceptions are representations of the patient's feelings and conceptions. This experience is different from that with the usual transference when the psychotherapist is more stably and more recognizably used to represent someone in the patient's life. Instead, the psychotherapist, working with the schizophrenic patient, may have the unpleasant sensation of being a figment of his patient's mind, a figure in his patient's dream, a twin image of the patient, a body the patient has entered to use in expressing himself. Similarly, the patient often represents through his actions and feelings how he sees the psychotherapist. That is, for the psychotherapist, like looking into a mirror, only half aware that he is doing so, and seeing what he cannot or does not want to recognize as himself. At such moments, the psychotherapist may find he wants to shatter the mirror. He is unreasonably annoyed with what he imagines is the kind of person the patient is.

All of this is made very complicated by the unwitting tendency of the psychotherapist and others to assume that the schizophrenic patient is using words to represent meanings in the same way he and they do, because the words sound the same and are even often strung together similarly.

I think it is possible that the tenuous nature of the relationship with the schizophrenic patient has more to do with the psychotherapist's (as well as others') intolerance of the experience of the actual modes of representation and communication used by the schizophrenic person, and their subsequent withdrawal from him, than with his lack of interest in such relationships.

On the whole, I find schizophrenic persons interested in reality and in others, but rather expecting to be misunderstood by, or to put off, others, and therefore uneasy as a foreigner might be who worries that he cannot make himself understood to a tribe of cannibals he has stumbled across.

If I feel a patient is a human being much like me, if I am moderately interested in working with him, and find him on occasion enjoyable to be around, chances are we will be able to work together. If I have phantasies—I include some theoretical notions here—indicating that I find the patient unusually strange, mysterious, attractive, wise, violent, wicked, saintly, large, or small, or I find myself taking a rather self-consciously professional stance, it is likely that I am worried by what he is representing and communicating, that I am working very hard to keep my distance, and that he will not find my withdrawal and aloofness, no matter how they are garbed, especially helpful; chances are we will probably not be able to work together. That, I should like to emphasize, is not necessarily because the patient has gone away from me or is not interested in reaching out and getting some reasonable care and understanding from someone.

There is one other thing you may notice about your schizophrenic patient. Each time he meets you, you may have a sense that he does not quite recognize you, that you have become a stranger to him since the last session, and that he has to set about somewhat laboriously to get to know you again. You will recognize after awhile the various maneuvers and movements he makes in order to become reacquainted; frequently, he may wait for you to say something or elicit some comment from you, perhaps through a question. Sometimes he may behave startlingly as though he has forgotten you completely—what you are like, what his experiences with you have been. You are suddenly an enemy. Apparently between sessions his image of you has altered— much for the worse, as far as you are concerned.

This is, I think, not necessarily to be understood as the result of an abandonment of objects and their representations in favor of an excessive cathexis of the self-representation. It is not paradoxical that with this apparent easy forgetting of you goes a dread of being separated from you. What is important here is that at the patient's level of organization and functioning, all symbolic representations, whether of self or object, are unstable. (You may recall Selma Fraiberg's impressive studies of congenitally blind infants—the difficulty such infants have in creating a constant or stable symbolic representation of external objects, which can be evoked in the absence of the object; their apparent difficulty in believing that others or anything continues to exist when tactile contact with them or it is interrupted; their painful response to separation, when the other is felt suddenly to disappear from existence, unrecallable, into a nameless void.)

I think that much of the process of psychotherapy with schizophrenic persons may have to do not only with changes in the conceptions symbolized in self-representation and object-representations but as well with the form of such representations and an increasing capacity of the patient to create and maintain a stable self-representation and stable object-representations. I have noticed that when my patient is able to remember me from session to session, to evoke an image of me in my absence that is reasonably like me and neither distorted nor frightening, to miss me when we are apart and to greet me with recognition, he is usually at the same time also beginning to feel that he knows from day to day who he is and what self continues through his experience. Then he is encouraged, and so am I.

I feel we have accomplished as much as we can for now. I am expressing my hope, as well as perhaps that of some of you, if I say at this point not "this is the end," but "to be continued when next we meet."

References

Lecture 1

Burke, Kenneth. *Permanence and Change.* New York: Bobbs-Merrill Co., 1954.
———. *Perspectives by Incongruity.* Bloomington: Indiana University Press, 1964.
———. *Language as Symbolic Action.* Berkeley: University of California Press, 1966.
———. *A Grammar of Motives.* Berkeley: University of California Press, 1969.
———. *A Rhetoric of Motives.* Berkeley: University of California Press, 1969.
Cassirer, Ernst. *An Essay on Man.* New Haven: Yale University Press, 1944.
———. *Language and Myth.* New York: Dover Publications, 1946.
———. *The Philosophy of Symbolic Forms.* New Haven: Yale University Press, 1953.
Freud, Sigmund. *The Standard Edition of the Complete Psychological Works of Sigmund Freud.* Edited by James Strachey. London: Hogarth Press, 1953-66.
Hartmann, Heinz. *Ego Psychology and the Problem of Adaptation.* New York: International Universities Press, 1958.
———. *Essays on Ego Psychology.* New York: International Universities Press, 1964.
Langer, Susanne. *Philosophy in a New Key.* New York: Penguin Books, 1948.
———. *Feeling and Form.* New York: Charles Scribner's Sons, 1953.
———. *Problems of Art.* New York: Charles Scribner's Sons, 1957.
Lévi-Strauss, Claude. *Structural Anthropology.* New York: Basic Books, 1963.
———. *Totemism.* Boston: Beacon Press, 1963.
———. *The Savage Mind.* Chicago: University of Chicago Press, 1966.
Parsons, Talcott. *The Structure of Social Action.* New York: Free Press of Glencoe, 1949.
———. "An Outline of the Social System," in *Theories of Society,* 1. Edited by Parsons et al. New York: Free Press of Glencoe, 1961.
———. *Toward a General Theory of Action.* New York: Harper Torchbook, 1962.
———. "Pattern Variables Revisited: A Response to Robert Dubin," in *Sociological Theory and Modern Society,* pp. 192-219. New York: Free Press, 1967.
Stevens, Wallace. "The Noble Rider and the Sound of Words," in *The Necessary Angel,* pp. 1-36. New York: Vintage Books, 1951.
———. "Adagia," in *Opus Posthumous,* pp. 157-80. New York: Alfred A. Knopf, 1966.

137

Lecture 2

Bertalanffy, Ludwig von. "An Outline of General System Theory," *British Journal for the Philosophy of Science* 1 (1950): 139-64.

Bleuler, Eugen. *Dementia Praecox.* New York: International Universities Press, 1950.

Cannon, Walter B. *The Wisdom of the Body.* New York: W. W. Norton, 1932.

Crookshank, F. G. "The Importance of a Theory of Signs and a Critique of Language in the Study of Medicine," in C. K. Ogden and I. A. Richards, *The Meaning of Meaning,* pp. 337-55. New York: Harcourt, Brace, and World, 1923.

Freud, Sigmund. "Three Essays on the Theory of Sexuality," *Standard Edition,* 7:123-245.

_____. "Psycho-analytic Notes on an Autobiographical Account of a Case of Paranoia," *Standard Edition,* 12:1-82.

_____. "Formulations on the Two Principles of Mental Functioning," *Standard Edition,* 12:213-26.

_____. "Types of Onset of Neurosis," *Standard Edition,* 12:227-38.

_____. "On Narcissism: An Introduction," *Standard Edition,* 14:67-102.

_____. "Instincts and Their Vicissitudes," *Standard Edition,* 14:109-40.

_____. "The Unconscious," *Standard Edition,* 14:159-215.

_____. "A Metapsychological Supplement to the Theory of Dreams," *Standard Edition,* 14:217-35.

_____. "Neurosis and Psychosis," *Standard Edition,* 19:147-53.

_____. "The Loss of Reality in Neurosis and Psychosis," *Standard Edition,* 19:181-87.

Hartmann, Heinz. *Essays on Ego Psychology.* New York: International Universities Press, 1964.

Isaacs, Susan. "The Nature and Function of Phantasy," in *Developments in Psycho-analysis,* pp. 67-121. Edited by Melanie Klein et al. London: Hogarth Press, 1952.

Kris, Ernst. "The Recovery of Childhood Memories in Psychoanalysis," *The Psychoanalytic Study of the Child,* 11:54-88. New York: International Universities Press, 1956.

Piaget, Jean. "The Role of the Concept of Equilibrium in Psychological Explication," in *Six Psychological Studies,* pp. 100-15. New York: Vintage Books, 1968.

Provence, Sally. "Some Aspects of Early Ego Development: Data from a Longitudinal Study," in *Psychoanalysis—A General Psychology,* pp. 107-22. Edited by Rudolph Loewenstein. New York: International Universities Press, 1966.

Schafer, Roy. "The Mechanisms of Defence." *International Journal of Psychoanalysis* 49 (1968): 49-62.

Sullivan, Harry Stack. "Peculiarity of Thought in Schizophrenia," in *Schizophrenia as a Human Process,* pp. 26-99. New York: W. W. Norton, 1962.

Lecture 3

Brown, Roger. *Words and Things.* New York: Free Press, 1958.

Cassirer, Ernst. *The Philosophy of Symbolic Forms.* Vol. 1, *Language.* New Haven: Yale University Press, 1953.

Federn, Paul. *Ego Psychology and the Psychoses.* New York: Basic Books, 1952.

Freud, Sigmund. *On Aphasia.* New York: International Universities Press, 1953.

————. "The Unconscious," *Standard Edition,* 14:161-215.

Hartmann, Heinz. "Contribution to the Metapsychology of Schizophrenia," in *Essays on Ego Psychology,* pp. 182-206. New York: International Universities Press, 1964.

Kris, Ernst. "Aesthetic Ambiguity," in *Psychoanalytic Explorations in Art,* pp. 243-64. New York: International Universities Press, 1952.

Langer, Susanne. *Philosophy in a New Key.* New York: Penguin Books, 1948.

————. *Feeling and Form.* New York: Charles Scribner's Sons, 1953.

————. *Problems of Art.* New York: Charles Scribner's Sons, 1957.

Lidz, Theodore. *The Family and Human Adaptation.* New York: International Universities Press, 1963.

Loewald, Hans. "Superego and Time," *International Journal of Psychoanalysis* 43 (1962): 264-68.

Ogden, C. K., and Richards, I. A. *The Meaning of Meaning.* New York: Harcourt, Brace, and World, 1923.

Parsons, Talcott. *The Social System.* New York: Free Press of Glencoe, 1951.

————. *Social Structure and Personality.* New York: Free Press of Glencoe, 1964.

————. *Sociological Theory and Modern Society.* New York: Free Press, 1967.

Pious, William. "Obsessive-Compulsive Symptoms in an Incipient Schizophrenia," *Psychoanalytic Quarterly* 19 (1950): 327-51.

————. "A Hypothesis about the Nature of Schizophrenic Behavior," in *Psychotherapy of the Psychoses,* pp. 43-68. Edited by Arthur Burton. New York: Basic Books, 1961.

Sapir, Edward. "Language," in *Culture, Language and Personality,* pp. 1-44. Berkeley: University of California Press, 1966.

Schafer, Roy. "The Loving and Beloved Superego in Freud's Structural Theory," in *The Psychoanalytic Study of the Child,* 15:163-88. New York: International Universities Press, 1960.

————. *Aspects of Internalization.* New York: International Universities Press, 1968.

Schur, Max. *The Id and the Regulatory Principles of Mental Functioning.* New York: International Universities Press, 1966.

Sullivan, Harry Stack. "The Language of Schizophrenia," in *Language and Thought in Schizophrenia,* pp. 4-16. Edited by J. S. Kasanin. Berkeley: University of California Press, 1944.

Thoreau, H. D. *Walden,* New York: Modern Library, 1937.

Whorf, Benjamin Lee. *Language, Thought and Reality.* Cambridge: M.I.T. Press, 1956.

Lecture 4

Federn, Paul. *Ego Psychology and the Psychoses.* New York: Basic Books, 1952.

[Fisher, Charles]. "Nightmares Compared to Temporary Psychotic Attacks." Special report in *Frontiers of Hospital Psychiatry* 6, no. 18 (1969): 1, 2, 11.

Fraiberg, Selma. "Parallel and Divergent Patterns in Blind and Sighted Infants," in *The Psychoanalytic Study of the Child,* 23:264-300. New York: International Universities Press, 1968.

Langer, Susanne. *Philosophy in a New Key.* New York: Penguin Books, 1948.

Lidz, Theodore, Stephen Fleck, and Alice Cornelison. *Schizophrenia and the Family.* New York: International Universities Press, 1965.

Pious, William. "A Hypothesis about the Nature of Schizophrenic Behavior," in *Psychotherapy of the Psychoses,* pp. 43-68. Edited by Arthur Burton. New York: Basic Books, 1961.

Whorf, Benjamin Lee. "Science and Linguistics," in *Language, Thought, and Reality,* pp. 207-19. Cambridge: M.I.T. Press, 1956.